New Mexico Marriages

Santo Tomás Apóstol de Abiquiú
Abiquiú, NM

1829 – 1837
1845 – 1853

Extracted & Transcribed

By

Members of the

New Mexico Genealogical Society

Published by

New Mexico Genealogical Society

Library of Congress Control Number: 2018940551

ISBN: 978-1-942626-66-4

Copyright © 2018

New Mexico Genealogical Society
P. O. Box 27559
Albuquerque, NM 87125

Table of Contents

Santo Tomás, Apóstol de Abiquiú Church Marriage Register

2 May 1829 – 21 March 1837
21 November 1845 – 16 October 1853

This publication of marriage extractions is from a marriage register of the Catholic mission church of Santo Tomás Apóstol de Abiquiú, Abiquiú, New Mexico. This and six other registers recently surfaced and were previously in private possession. These parish registers were entrusted to the Center for Southwest Research (CSWR) at the Zimmerman Library, University of New Mexico, for analysis, preservation, microfilming and extraction for public access. The CSWR also assisted in transferring these registers to the Archives of the Archdiocese of Santa Fe (AASF).

Archbishop Rudolph Aloysius Gerken assembled the AASF in 1933. These recently recovered Abiquiú church registers were not included in *fray* Angélico Chávez' inventory of ancient sacramental books and documents, *Archives of the Archdiocese of Santa Fe, 1678-1900,* published in 1957. The microfilm taken of these registers are catalogued and available for public viewing at the CSWR. The Santo Tomás, Apóstol de Abiquiú Church registers that are part of this CSWR and New Mexico Genealogical Society (NMGS) recovery and extraction project are:

- Baptisms: 1 Jan 1812 – 24 Feb 1821; 17 Jan 1829 – 3 May 1832; 8 Sep 1842 – 23 Apr 1848; 19 Jan 1852 – 20 Dec 1861.
- Marriages: 2 May 1829 – 16 Oct 1853.
- Burials: 22 Mar 1777 – 3 May 1827; 20 Jan 1829 – 23 Feb 1861.

These marriages will provide many connections that have been missing from the written record in terms of family history. Written in all the flourish of the priest who administered and oversaw the marriages, these records provide first and last names in variant spellings, neighboring towns and villages where the families resided, and gives information about parents, godparents and witnesses to the marriages. The records also note if a person was married previously with information about deceased spouses.

The extractions herein contain pertinent information in Spanish with English translations used for more detailed information. Surnames are written as they appear. Accent marks are inconsistent in the original entries therefore, they are primarily omitted in this work. The names of the priests who administered the marriages or visited the parish are not noted in this extraction work. Examination of the microfilm is necessary to study the pastoral administration of Santo Tomás Apóstol Church, the priests' terms of residency and episcopal and/or ecclesial visitations. The NMGS does not claim 100% accuracy in its extractions nor did they extract other church annotations or anecdotal information. Researchers are responsible for verifying the information with the original register or the microfilmed copy.

Acknowledgements

The New Mexico Genealogical Society is pleased to publish this book of marriages found in registers from the Mission Church at Abiquiú. One of the purposes of our organization is to publish various New Mexico records for the benefit of those studying history and family genealogy. The extractions are made as near to the original document as possible so that the researcher may make his or her own interpretations of the record. Errors brought to our attention will be corrected in the New Mexico Genealogist.

Other Abiquiú church records were extracted in the late 1990s and are available to the public. It is the goal of the NMGS to extract, transcribe and make available historical information to the public in a manner that is easily accessible and useful. We wish to acknowledge and thank the many volunteers who worked on this laborious and time intensive project who are: Samuel Sisneros, Henrietta Martinez Christmas, Nancy Anderson, Dannette Burch, Patricia Wallace, Danny Martinez, Terri Carlson, Angela Lewis and Miguel Torrez.

Abbreviations/Glossary

NS – means no surname

s/ - son of

d/ - daughter of

D. – Don or *don*

ch/ - children of

am/ - maternal grandparents

famula – in this case we used servant, but can mean from the household

legit - legitimate

ap/ - paternal grandparents

b. – born

gp/ - godparents

vecino(a) – neighbor, of that place, resident, in good standing within a community. Sometimes synonymous with "Spanish" or of the Spanish class or category but not always.

Items underlined = typed as shown.

• Canjilon

• Placita Garcia

Rio Colorado

Rio del Ojo Caliente

El Rito •
Las Placitas •

• Ojo Caliente

Rio Chama

• Plaza Colorado

Youngsville •   Barranca •   ⊙   • La Puente

Abiquiu   • Terra Azul

Cañones •

• Medanales

• Coyote

• Arroyo del Aqua

Rio del Oso

Chili •

La Cuchilla •

Hernandez •   • San Juan Pueblo

San Jose •

Española •   • Santa Cruz

Santa Clara Pueblo •

Rio Grande

Photo #069910 - T. Harmon Parkhurst - Ruins, Santa Rosa de Lima church, Abiquiu, New Mexico. Fray Angelico Chavez Photo Archives, Santa Fe, New Mexico

Marriage Register 2 May 1829 – 21 March 1837

2 May 1829 – **Jose Maria Chaves**, of the Plaza of San Francisco, legit s/ Francisco Antonio Chaves and Rosalia Berlarde, m. **Maria de Jesus Martin**, of the Plaza of San Francisco, legit d/ Manuel Martin and Maria Manuela Quintana; pad/ Jose Francisco Vigil and Maria Dolores Lopes; wit/ Juan Antonio Gonzales, Juliana Baldes, Ramon Ruibali and Eugenio Naranjo. (pg 1)

2 May 1829 – **Jose Eucebio Martin**, of la Puente, legit s/ Manuel Martin and Maria Manuela Quintana, m. **Maria Josefa Chaves,** both residents of la Puente, legit d/ Francisco Antonio Chaves and Rosalia Belarde; pad/ Jose Chaves and Maria Dolores Martin, married couple, both residents of San Miguel of la Puente; wit/ Mateo Garcia, Miguel Atencio, Manuel Martin and Jose Rafael Duran. (pg 1)

7 Jun 1829 – **Manuel Rafael Martin**, of the Plaza of San Antonio of el Rito, legit s/ Manuel Lorenzo Martin and Antonia [illegible], m. **Maria Marina Romana Martin**, of the Plaza of San Antonio of el Rito, legit d/ Jose Cristoval Martin and Gertrudes[torn]; pad/ Don Jose Maria Ortiz and Doña Ysadora Ortiz, residents of the Plaza of San Antonio of el Rito; wit/ Jose Manuel Montoya, Miguel Antonio Gallego, Marco Garcia and Ysidro Antonio Gallego. (pg 1)

10 Jul 1829 – **Juan Pedro de Herrera**, of Ojo Caliente, legit s/ Jose Antonio de Herrera and Maria Luisa Medina, m. **Maria Manuela Griego**, of Ojo Caliente, legit d/ Juan de Jesus Griego and Maria Soledad Griego; pad/ Juan Reyes Sena and Maria de la Luz Sena, residents of the Plaza of Santa Cruz of Ojo Caliente; wit/ Bentura Manzanares, Manuel Garcia, Pedro Lujan and Antonio Gutierres. (pg 2b)

19 Sep 1829 – **Juan de Jesus Garcia**, of Abiquiu, legit s/ Miguel Garcia and Barbara Antonia Truxillo, m. **Rosita Romero**, of Abiquiu, legit d/ Jose Antonio Romero and Maria de la Luz Chacon; pad/ Antonio Gutierres and Maria Ygnacia Benavedes, residents of Santo Tomas Apostol of Abiquiu; wit/ Domingo Martin, Juan Jose Martin, Juan Cristobal Martin and Pedro Antonio Fernandes. (pg 2b)

19 Sep 1829 – **Juan Antonio Martin**, of Abiquiu, widower of Joaquina Duran, m. **Juana Gertrudis Martin**, of Abiquiu, legit d/ Manuel Martin and Maria Atanacia Truxillo; pad/ Jose Pablo Truxillo and Maria de Jesus Lujan, residents of Santo Tomas Apostol of Abiquiu; wit/ Jose Pablo Truxillo, Juan Gutierres, Ygnacio Truxillo and Juan Jose Martin. (pg 3)

27 Sep 1829 – **Francisco Manzanares**, of the Plaza of San Miguel of la Puente, legit s/ Juan Cristobal Manzanares and Maria Francisca Martin, m. **Maria Consepcion Serda**, of the Plaza of San Miguel of la Puente, legit d/ Domingo Serda and Maria Manuela Martin; pad/ Francisco

Martin and Maria Dolores Martin, residents of the plaza of San Miguel of la Puente; wit/ Rafael Baldes, Juan Luiz Mestes, Jose Manuel Baldes and Jose Martin. (pg 3)

27 Sep 1829 – **Jose Sabino Chaves**, of the Plaza of San Juan Nepomuceno of el Rito Colorado, legit s/ Domingo Chaves and Antonia Vigil, m. **Maria Antonia Baldes**, of the Plaza of San Juan Nepomuceno of el Rito Colorado, legit d/ German Baldes and Maria Josefa Gomes; pad/ Manuel Gregorio Martin and Maria Inez Baldes, residents of the Plaza of San Juan Nepomuceno of el Rito; wit/ Jose Paulo Montoya, Antonio Martin, Antonio Jose Beita and Jose Miguel Archuleta. (pg 3/3b)

27 Sep 1829 – **Jose Francisco Baldes**, of the Plaza de Nuestra Señora Guadalupe of la Cueva, widower of 1st marriage to Maria Ygnacia Chaves, m. **Maria Jacinta Truxillo**, of the Plaza de Nuestra Señora Guadalupe of la Cueva, legit d/ Jose Juan Truxillo and Maria Luisa Gallegos; pad/ Jose Rafael Baldes and Maria Juana Chaves, residents of the Plaza de Nuestra Señora Guadalupe of la Cueva; wit/ Jose Ramon Lopes, Salvador Pineda, Jose Antonio Espinosa and Diego Antonio Gomez. (pg 3b)

28 Sep 1829 – **Jose Ramon Salazar**, of the Plaza of San Juan Nepomuseno of el Rito, legit s/ Ylario Salazar and Maria Brigida Truxillo, m. **Maria Teodora Lopes**, of the Plaza of San Juan Nepomuseno of el Rito, legit d/ Ramon Lopes and Maria Lugarda Espinosa; pad/ Miguel Truxillo and Maria Barbara Truxillo, residents of the Plaza de Nuestra Señora Guadalupe of la Cueva; wit/ Mariano Serda, Jose Francisco Baldes, Jose de Jesus Chaves and Jose Julian Martin. (pg 3b)

3 Oct 1829 – **Tomas Chaves**, of the Ute nation of the Plaza of San Rafael purchased by Antonio Chaves, deceased, m. **Maria Andrea Jaramillo**, of the Plaza of San Rafael, legit d/ Jose Antonio Jaramillo and Rafaela Jaramillo; pad/ Jose Maria del Socorro Chaves and Maria Teodora Salome Chaves, residents of the Plaza of San Rafael; wit/ Jose Rafael Truxillo, Profiro Trujillo, Domingo Martin and Santiago Ydalgo. (pg 4)

2 Nov 1829 – **Juan Pio Baldes**, of the Plaza of San Rafael, legit s/ Jose Manuel Baldes and Maria Paula Ruibali, m. **Maria Nestora Salazar**, of the Plaza of San Rafael, legit d/ Jose Manuel Salazar and Biviana Sisneros; pad/ Antonio Jose Baldes and Maria Soledad Martin, residents of the Plaza of San Rafael; wit/ Jose Ysidro Baldes, Pedro Truxillo, Juan Gutierres and Julian Madrid. (pg 4)

10 Nov 1829 – **Concepcion Lucero**, of the Plaza of Santa Cruz of Ojo Caliente, legit s/ Pedro Antonio Lucero and Maria Francisca Maez, m. **Maria de la Luz Sena**, of the Plaza of Santa Cruz of Ojo Caliente, legit d/ Juan de los Reyes Sena and Maria Joaquina Chaves; pad/ Juan Jose

Olguin and Maria Paula Rodrigues, residents of Santa Cruz of Ojo Caliente; wit/ Juan de Jesus Serna, Jose Antonio Suazo, Noberto Naranjo and Manuel Antonio Quintana. (pg 4)

20 Nov 1829 – **Antonio de Jesus Trugillo**, of the Plaza of Santa Cruz of Ojo Caliente, widower of 1st marriage to Juana Quintana, m. **Maria Manuela Jaques**, of the Plaza of Santa Cruz of Ojo Caliente, legit d/ Felipe Jaques and Maria Micaela Chaves; pad/ Jose de la Cruz Baldes and Maria Manuela Salazar, residents of Santa Cruz of Ojo Caliente; wit/ Jose Antonio Miera, Candelario Ruibali, Eugenio Naranjo and Juan Gutierres. (pg 4b)

28 Nov 1829 – **Ramon Candelario Lopes**, of the Plaza of Santa Cruz of Ojo Caliente, legit s/ Miguel Antonio Lopes and Maria Josefa Martin, m. **Maria Rafaela Martin**, of the Plaza of Santa Cruz of Ojo Caliente, legit d/ Manuel Lorenzo Martin and Maria Jesusa Lopes; pad/ Juan Jose Olgin and Maria Paula Rodrigues; wit/ Pedro Truxillo, Jose Antonio Madrid, Rafael Truxillo and Juan Agustin Chaves. (pg 4b)

29 Nov 1829 – **Juan de Jesus Ruivali**, of the Plaza de Nuestra Señora Guadalupe, legit s/ Juan de Jesus Ruivali and Maria Toribia Martin, m. **Maria Rosalia Gurule**, of the Plaza de Nuestra Señora Guadalupe, legit d/ Juan Antonio Gurule and Maria Antonia Maes; pad/ Tomas de Jesus Chacon and Maria Candelaria Ruivali; wit/ Ysidro Martin and Juan de Jesus Garcia. (pg 4b/5)

30 Nov 1829 – **Juan Ysidro Trugillo**, of the Plaza de Nuestra Señora Guadalupe, legit s/ Agustin Trugillo and Maria Gertrudes Sisneros, m. **Maria de la Cruz Samora**, of the Plaza de Nuestra Señora Guadalupe, legit d/ Juan Samora, deceased, and Maria Manuela Lujan; pad/ Juan Martin and Trenidad Baldes; wit/ Domingo Martin and Rafael Trugillo. (pg 5)

2 Nov 1829 – **Antonio de la Cruz Baldes**, of Santa Cruz of Ojo Caliente, legit s/ Jose Eusebio Baldes and Maria Dolores Chaves, m. **Maria Manuela Lovato**, of Santa Cruz of Ojo Caliente, legit d/ Juan Pedro Lovato and Maria Josefa de los Reyes Samora; pad/ Diego Baldes and Maria de la Luz Balasques, residents of Santa Cruz of Ojo Caliente; wit/ Noberto Naranjo and Salvador Salasar. (pg 5)

5 Dec 1829 – **Felipe Neri Naranjo**, of Abiquiu s/ Maria Dolores Naranjo, m. **Maria Tomasa Casimira Vigil**, of Abiquiu, legit d/ Grabriel Vigil, deceased, and Anamaria Lucero; pad/ Martin de Jesus Martin and Maria Manuela Baldes, residents of Abiquiu; wit/ Jose Antonio Suaso and Manuel Gregorio Salas. (pg 5/5b)

2 Jan 1830 – **Manuel Antonio Trugillo**, of Abiquiu, widower of Maria de Jesus Garcia, m. **Maria Casilda Guillen**, of Abiquiu, widow of Agustin Ortiz; pad/ Asencio Espinosa and Maria Manuela Pando, residents of Abiquiu; wit/ Felipe Santiago Garcia and Jose Manuel Trugillo. (pg 5b)

10 Jan 1830 – **Miguel Antonio Mestas**, of Santa Cruz of Ojo Caliente, legit s/ Jose Antonio Mestas and Maria Rosa Trujillo, m. **Maria Josefa Samora**, of Santa Cruz of Ojo Caliente, legit d/ Francisco Samora and Maria Concepcion Uribali; pad/ Diego Antonio Lucero and Maria Theodora Gallego, residents of Santa Cruz of Ojo Caliente; wit/ Jose Visente Jaramillo and Jose Ramon Luxan. (pg 5b)

15 Jan 1830 – **Felipe Cordova**, of Santa Cruz of Ojo Caliente, legit s/ Manuel Cordova and Maria Luisa Ruibali, m. **Maria Soledad Jaques**, of Santa Cruz of Ojo Caliente, legit d/ Juan Manuel Jaques, deceased, and Maria Viviana Baldes; pad/ Pedro Antonio Lovato and Maria Conscepcion de Herrera, residents of Santa Cruz of Ojo Caliente; wit/ Jose Lucero and Mateo Romero. (pg 6)

24 Jan 1830 – **Antonio Aban Duran**, of Abiquiu, legit s/ Pablo Duran and Maria de Jesus Baldes, m. **Maria Teodora Gallego**, of Abiquiu, legit d/ Jose Ygnacio Gallego, deceased, and Maria Dorotea Garcia, deceased; pad/ Bernardo Baldes and Maria Rafaela Baldes, residents of Abiquiu; wit/ Antonio Domingo Trugillo and Maria de Jesus Martin. (pg 6)

24 Jan 1830 – **Ysidro Pasqual Sanches**, resident of the Plaza of San Miguel de Los Cañones s/ Ylaria de Jesus Sanches, m. **Maria Tomasa Casimira Romero**, resident of the Plaza of San Miguel de Los Cañones, legit d/ Luis Romero and Francisca Madrid; pad/ Juan Antonio Trugillo and Maria Rosa Vigil, all residents of the Plaza of San Miguel de Los Cañones; wit/ Protero Trugillo, Jose Ypolito Jaramillo and Jose Manuel Trugillo. (pg 6)

24 Jan 1830 – **Jose Guadalupe Galbes**, resident of Santa Cruz of Ojo Caliente, legit s/ Felipe Galbes and Maria Josefa Garcia, deceased, m. **Maria Barbara Baldes**, resident of Santa Cruz of Ojo Caliente, legit d/ Ygnacio Baldes and Maria Antonia Martin; pad/ Vicente Ferrer Maes and Maria Juliana Paes, all residents of Santa Cruz of Ojo Caliente; wit/ Rafael Trugillo and Geronimo Gallego. (pg 6b)

24 Jan 1830 – **Jose Julian Martin**, of Santa Cruz of Ojo Caliente, legit s/ Antonio Martin and Maria de la Cruz Gallego, m. **Maria Ynes Martin**, of Santa Cruz of Ojo Caliente, widow of Jose Juan Galbes; pad/ Rafael Baca and Bibiana Martin, residents of Santa Cruz of Ojo Caliente; wit/ Antonio Domingo Trugillo and Jose Rafael Trugillo. (pg 6b)

4 Feb 1830 – **Juan Pasqual Martin**, of the jurisdiction of Taos, legit s/ Seberino Martin and Maria del Carmel Santiestevan, both deceased, m. **Maria Teodora Gallego**, of the jurisdiction of Taos, legit d/ Miguel Antonio Gallego and Maria Rumalda Luzero; pad/ Pablo Lucero and Maria Ygnaca Lusero, residents of the jurisdiction of Taos; wit/ Manuel Baldes and Jose Ramon Ruibal. (pg 6b)

7 Feb 1830 – **Jose Mariano de Jesus Alarid**, resident of the plaza of San Miguel of la Puente, legit s/ Manuel Alarid, deceased, and Maria Josefa Ortiz, m. **Maria de la Luz Santiestevan**, resident of the plaza of San Miguel of la Puente, legit d/ Julian Santiestevan and Maria Encarnacion Martin, deceased; pad/ Marcos Ortiz and Maria Guadalupe Alarid, all residents of the plaza of San Miguel of la Puente; wit/ Juan Domingo Martin and Juan Agustin Chaves. (pg 7)

12 Apr 1830 – **Pedro Leon Lugan**, resident of Abiquiu, widower of Maria Manuela Garcia, m. **Ana Maria Jaramillo**, resident of Santo Tomas Apostol of Abiquiu, legit d/ Juan Agustin Jaramillo, deceased, and Maria de los Reyes Baldes; pad/ Lorenso Lucero and Maria Rufina Salasar, all residents of Santo Tomas Apostol of Abiquiu; wit/ Jose Maria Trugillo and Juan Francisco Garcia. (pg 7)

12 Apr 1830 – **Mariano Antonio Chaves**, of Abiquiu, legit s/ Francisco Antonio Chaves, deceased, and Rosalia Belarde, m. **Maria Luisa Gonzales**, of Santo Tomas Apostal of Abiquiu, legit d/ Jose Gonzales and Maria Guadalupe Beita; pad/ Faustin Montaño and Encarnacion Belarde, residents of Santo Tomas Apostal of Abiquiu; wit/ Jose Maria Trugillo and Juan Francisco Garcia. (pg 7/7b)

13 Apr 1830 – **Juan de Jesus Gallego**, of Abiquiu, legit s/ Felipe Santiago Gallego and Maria Rafaela Trugillo, deceased, m. **Maria Encarnacion Gutierres**, of Abiquiu, legit d/ Juan Gutierres and Guadalupe Martin; pad/ Bernardo Muñis and Barbara Montoya, residents of Santo Tomas Apostal of Abiquiu; wit/ Domingo Martin and Ysidro Martin. (pg 7b)

9 Aug 1830 – **Joaquin Gutierres**, of Abiquiu, legit s/ Pasqual Gutierres and Maria de la Merced Aguero, m. **Maria Juana Gonzales**, of Abiquiu, legit d/ Juan Antonio Gonzales and Maria Concepcion Martin; pad/ Miguel Chaves and Maria de la Luz Chaves, residents of Santo Tomas Apostal of Abiquiu; wit/ Antonio Domingo Trugillo and Juan Agustin Chaves. (pg 7b)

23 Aug 1830 – **Francisco Esteban Garcia de Luna**, of Abiquiu s/ Juana de Luna, m. **Maria Santa Martin**, of Abiquiu d/ Maria Roza Martin; pad/ Jose Pablo Gallego and Maria de la Atencio [cut off] Gallego, residents of Santo Tomas Apostal of Abiquiu; wit/ Jose Rafael Rodrigues and Grabriel Espinosa. (pg 7b/8)

31 Aug 1830 – **Baltasar Baca**, of Abiquiu, legit s/ Rafael Baca and Maria Antonia Gutierres, m. **Maria Teodora Gallego**, of Abiquiu, legit d/ Jose Gallego and Victoria Paes, deceased; pad/ Jose Gallego and Paula Baca, residents of Abiquiu; wit/ Antonio Domingo Trugillo and Agustin Chaves. (pg 8b)

6 Sep 1830 – **Jose Antonio Martin**, of Abiquiu, legit s/ Christobal Martin and Josefa Naranjo, m. **Maria Rutila Martin**, of Abiquiu, legit d/ Santiago Martin and Maria de la Cruz Baldes; pad/ Miguel Antonio Beita and Josefa Beita, residents of Abiquiu; wit/ Jose Pablo Trugillo and Miguel Antonio Gutierres. (pg 8b)

10 Sep 1830 – **Juan Jose Jaramillo**, of Abiquiu, legit s/ Juan Manuel Jaramillo and Feliciana Baldes, m. **Maria Josefa Martin**, of Abiquiu, legit d/ Juan de Jesus Martin and Maria de la Lus Atencio; pad/ Jose Manuel Delgado and Maria Josefa Delgado, residents of Abiquiu; wit/ Santiago Gallego and Jose Miguel Lugan. (pg 8b/9)

12 Sep 1830 – **Francisco Martin**, of this jurisdiction, legit s/ Juan Rosalio Martin and Josefa Mansanares, m. **Maria Rosalia Galbis**, of this jurisdiction, legit d/ Felipe Galbis, deceased, and Josefa Garcia, deceased; pad/ Manuel Gregorio Mansanares and Ana Maria Mansanares, residents of Abiquiu; wit/ Faustin Montaño and Mariano Trugillo. (pg 9)

19 Sep 1830 – **Jose Ramon Cordova**, of Santa Cruz of Ojo Caliente, widower of Maria Soledad Baldes, deceased, m. **Maria Antonia Quintana**, of Santa Cruz of Ojo Caliente, legit d/ Baltasar Quintana and Maria Manuela Martin; pad/ Juan Olgin and Paubla Rodriges, residents of Santa Cruz of Ojo Caliente; wit/ Jose Antonio Martin and Martin de Jesus Martin. (pg 9)

25 Sep 1830 – Antonio Jose de la Serda, of Abiquiu, legit s/ Domingo Serda and Manuela Martin, m. Maria Luteria Mestas, of Abiquiu, legit d/ Jose Maria Maestas and Maria Dolores Rodrigues; pad/ Jose Manuel Ribera and Dolores Garcia, residents of Abiquiu; wit/ Lorenzo Trugillo and Diego Antonio Gonsales. (pg 9b)

28 Sep 1830 – **Juan Antonio Alire**, of Santa Cruz of Ojo Caliente, legit s/ Tomas Antonio Alire and Maria Francisca Rodriges, m. **Maria Manuela Baldes**, of Santa Cruz of Ojo Caliente, legit d/ Nicolas Baldes, deceased, and Maria Ysabel Martin; pad/ Jose Julian Martin and Maria Ygnes Martin, residents of Santa Cruz of Ojo Caliente; wit/ Candelario Archuleta and Paublo Agiliar (pg 9b)

28 Sep 1830 – **Juan Jose Duran**, of this jurisdiction, widower of Maria Dolores Olgin, deceased, m. **Maria Rita Baldes**, of this jurisdiction, legit d/ Santiago Baldes and Maria Getrudis Gallegos; pad/ Nepomuceno Baca and Guadalupe Baca, residents of Abiquiu; wit/ Candelario Archuleta and Paubla Agilar. (pg 10)

9 Oct 1830 – **Manuel Lorenzo Baldes**, of this jurisdiction, legit s/ Mariano Baldes and Manuela Casias, m. **Maria Patrocinia Duran**, of this jurisdiction, legit d/ Visente Duran and Maria Juana Belasques; pad/ Nepomuceno Trugillo and Consecion Ruibal, residents of the Plaza of Santa Cruz of Ojo Caliente; wit/ Domingo Martin and Rafael Baldes. (pg 10)

17 Oct 1830 – **Domingo Madrid**, of this jurisdiction, s/ Reyes Madrid, deceased, m. **Maria Teodora Martin**, of this jurisdiction, legit d/ Juan Francisco Martin and Maria Ygnacia Baldes; pad/ Francisco Antonio Archuleta and Barbara Lopes, residents of Abiquiu; wit/ Pablo Romero and Juan Christobal Madrid. (pg 10b)

17 Oct 1830 – **Manuel Gregorio Serrano**, of this jurisdiction, legit s/ Ypolito Serrano and Maria Dolores Martin, m. **Maria Manuela Martin**, of this jurisdiction, legit d/ Juan Pedro Martin, deceased, and Maria Cerafaina Trugillo; pad/ Bernardo Muñis and Barbara Montolla, residents of Abiquiu; wit/ Pablo Romero and Juan Christobal Madrid. (pg 10b)

24 Oct 1830 – **Juan de Jesus Gonsales**, of this jurisdiction, widower of Juana Maria Belasques, m. **Maria Cecilia Atencio**, of this jurisdiction, legit d/ Juan Ygnacio Atencio and Maria Rosa Padilla; pad/ Alejandro Torres and Maria de Refugio Martin, residents of Abiquiu; wit/ Jose Antonio Suaso and Manuel Lorenso Trugillo. (pg 11)

31 Oct 1830 – **Francisco Martin**, of this jurisdiction, legit s/ Juan de Dios Martin, deceased, and Maria Antonia Garcia, deceased, m. **Maria Manuela Trugillo**, of this jurisdiction, legit d/ Domingo Trugillo and Juana Getrudes Patrona; pad/ Pedro Antonio Trugillo and Maria Romuela Trugillo, residents of Abiquiu; wit/ Ygnacio Trugillo and Mariano Trugillo. (pg 11)

7 Nov 1830 – **Diego Antonio Espinosa**, of this jurisdiction, legit s/ Francisco Espinosa and Maria Antonia Quintana, m. **Maria Rita Baldes**, of this jurisdiction, legit d/ German Baldes and Maria Josefa Gomes; pad/ Francisco Estevan Vigil and Maria Alcadia Salazar, residents of Abiquiu; wit/ Manuel Mansanares and Miguel Segura. (pg 11b)

11 Nov 1830 – **Casimiro Madrid**, of this jurisdiction, legit s/ Antonio Jose Madrid and Maria Josefa Atencio, m. **Maria Rosalia Gallego**, of this jurisdiction, legit d/ Domingo Gallego and Maria Consepcion Gallegos; pad/ Diego Madrid and Maria Pamuela Jaramillo, residents of Abiquiu; wit/ Atencio Trugillo and Antonio Muños. (pg 11b)

26 Nov 1830 – **Gregorio de Jesus Atencio**, of this jurisdiction, legit s/ Miguel Asencio Atencio and Maria Manuela Martin, m. **Maria Guadalupe Lusero**, of this jurisdiction, legit d/ Miguel Lusero, deceased, and Maria de la Lus Martin; pad/ Tomas de Jesus Chacon and Maria de los Reyes Baldes, residents of Abiquiu; wit/ Juan de Jesus Lusero and Jose Miguel Jaramillo. (pg 12)

11 Dec 1830 – **Tomas Chaves**, of this jurisdiction, widower of Juana Martin, deceased, m. **Maria de los Reyes Baldes**, of this jurisdiction, widow of Juan Agustin Jaramillo, deceased;

pad/ Lorenso Trugillo and Dolores Archuleta, residents of Abiquiu; wit/ Francisco Marques and Antonio Muños. (pg 12)

11 Dec 1830 – **Felipe Santiago Espinosa**, of this jurisdiction, widower of Maria Asencion Lugan, deceased, m. **Maria Juliana Ruibal**, of this jurisdiction, widow of Miguel Ramires, deceased; pad/ Antonio Espinosa and Dolores Archuleta, residents of Abiquiu; wit/ Jose Rafael Duran and Jose Maria Trugillo. (pg 12)

18 Dec 1830 – **Jose Modesto Trugillo**, of this jurisdiction, s/ Maria del Rosario Trugillo, m. **Maria Soledad Olgin**, of this jurisdiction, legit d/ Christobal Olgin, deceased, and Josefa Belasques; pad/ Lorenso Trugillo and Dolores Archuleta, residents of Abiquiu; wit/ Culas Lugan and Jose Maria Garcia. (pg 12b)

19 Dec 1830 – **Juan Noverto Trugillo**, of this jurisdiction, widower of 1st marriage to Maria Alta Gracia Vigil, m. **Maria Paubla Torres**, of this jurisdiction, legit d/ Bernardo Torres and Maria Getrudis Jaques; pad/ Francisco Baldes and Dolores Trugillo, residents of Abiquiu; wit/ Jose Manuel Trugillo and Nicolas Trugillo. (pg 12b)

30 Dec 1830 – **Antonio Eugenio Ortiz**, of this jurisdiction, legit s/ Esteban Ortiz and Maria Ygnacia Sisneros, m. **Maria Rita Mestas**, of this jurisdiction, legit d/ Juan Simon Mestas and Maria de Jesus Balberde; pad/ Gregorio Jaramillo and Loreta Trugillo, residents of Abiquiu; wit/ Mariano Trugillo and Nicolas Trugillo. (pg 13)

1 Jan 1831 – **Jose Ygnacio Moya**, of this jurisdiction, legit s/ Antonio Jose Moya and Maria Nicolasa Armijo, deceased, m. **Maria Rufina Martin**, of this jurisdiction, legit d/ Paublo Martin, deceased, and Maria Gertrudis Lopes; pad/ Jose Paublo Trugillo and Joaquina Moya, residents of Abiquiu; wit/ Domingo Trugillo and Antonio Gutierres. (pg 13)

2 Jan 1831 – **Jose Santiago Garcia de la Mora**, of this jurisdiction, legit s/ Atencio de Jesus Garcia de la Mora and Maria Josefa Tafoya, m. **Tomasa Martin**, of this jurisdiction, legit d/ Jose Martin and Maria Rita Villapando; pad/ Jose Antonio Martin and Consecion Olgin, residents of Abiquiu; wit/ Visente Trugillo and Jose de la Cruz Trugillo. (pg 13b)

15 Jan 1831 – **Jose Maria Chacon**, of this jurisdiction, legit s/ Ygnacio Chacon, deceased, and Maria Pasquela Martin, m. **Maria Serafina Lopes**, of this jurisdiction, legit d/ Miguel Lopes and Maria Manuela Mestas; pad/ Julian Martin and Caterina Ortiz, residents of Abiquiu; wit/ Manuel Marques and Pedro Peña. (pg 13b)

16 Jan 1831 – **Juan de Jesus Martin**, of this jurisdiction, legit s/ Juan Rosalio Martin and Juana Maria de Jesus Peña, m. **Maria Barbara Marques**, of this jurisdiction, legit d/ Manuel Marques

and Maria Manuela Lucsero; pad/ Jesus Maria Varela and Maria Nicolasa Gallego, residents of Abiquiu; wit/ Ysidro Martin and Tomas Chacon. (pg 14)

19 Jan 1831 – **Manuel de los Dolores Trugillo**, of this jurisdiction, legit s/ Jose Juan Trugillo, deceased, and Maria Luisa Gallego, m. **Maria Rita Torres**, of this jurisdiction, legit d/ Jose Bernardo Torres and Maria Gertrudis Jaques; pad/ Manuel Rafael Martin and Mariana Muñis, residents of Abiquiu; wit/ Ramon Martin and Francisco Antonio Martin. (pg 14)

13 Feb 1831 – **Jose Mariano Serda**, of this jurisdiction, widower of Vibiana Balberde, deceased, m. **Maria Pasquala Trugillo**, of this jurisdiction, widow of Pedro Martin, deceased; pad/ Miguel Baldes and Rosalia Atencio, residents of Abiquiu; wit/ Juan Bautista Trugillo and Lorenso Trugillo. (pg 14b)

19 Feb 1831 – **Francisco Antonio Torres**, of this jurisdiction, legit s/ Manuel Gregorio Torres and Maria Antonia Espinosa, m. **Maria Serafina Casados**, of this jurisdiction, legit d/ Jose Ygnacio Casados and Vitorina Lopes; pad/ Bernardo Muñis and Barbara Montoya, residents of Abiquiu; wit/ Franciso Antonio Martin and Profiro Trugillo. (pg 14b)

19 Feb 1831 – **Pedro Antonio Baldes**, of this jurisdiction, legit s/ Jose Miguel Baldes and Maria Francisca Mastas, m. **Maria Conspecion Garcia**, of this jurisdiction, legit d/ Sisto Garcia and Maria de los Reyes Lobato, deceased; pad/ Pedro Antonio Lovato and Manuela Herrera, residents of Abiquiu; wit/ Juan Agustin Chabes and Juan de Jesus Gallego. (pg 15)

26 Feb 1831 – **Juan Antonio Chaves**, of this jurisdiction, legit s/ Juan Christobal Chabes and Barbara Antonia Gallego, deceased, m. **Encarnacion Lusero**, of this jurisdiction, legit d/ Manuel Lusero and Casilda Mestas; pad/ Jose Antonio Sanches and Maria de Jesus Mascareñas, residents of Abiquiu; wit/ Rafael Baca and Juan Agustin Chabes. (pg 15)

13 Mar 1831 – **Jose Ramon Atencio**, of this jurisdiction, widower of Antonia Rosalia Sanches, deceased, m. **Maria de la Lus Archuleta**, of this jurisdiction, widow of Juan Chabes, deceased; pad/ Jose Manuel Atencio and Maria Lucia Mestes, residents of Abiquiu; wit/ Salbador Trugillo and Juan Garviso. (pg 15b)

27 Mar 1831 – **Antonio Jose Quintana**, of this jurisdiction, widower of Maria Juliana Sisneros, deceased, m. **Maria Guadalupe Trugillo**, of this jurisdiction, legit d/ Francisco Trugillo and Maria Getrudis Martin; pad/ Diego de Luna and Catarina Sanches, residents of Abiquiu; wit/ Eugenio Naranjo and Salbador Gonsales. (pg 15b)

23 Apr 1831 – **Manuel de Jesus Urribali**, of this jurisdiction, legit s/ Gregorio Uraibali, deceased, and Josefa Mansanares, m. **Maria Francisca Gomes**, of this jurisdiction, legit d/

Felipe Gomes and Maria de la Lus Martin; pad/ Jose Urribali and Maria Josefa Martin, residents of Abiquiu; wit/ Santiago Gallego and Juan Gutierres. (pg 15b/16)

24 Apr 1831 – **Juan Francisco Archuleta**, of this jurisdiction, legit s/ Nicolas Archuleta and Maria Candelaria Martin, m. **Maria de las Nieves Baldes**, of this jurisdiction, legit d/ Jose Miguel Baldes and Maria Francisca Mestas; pad/ Thomas Chacon and Maria de los Reyes Baldes, residents of Abiquiu; wit/ Rafael Baca and Salvador Gonsales. (pg 16)

30 Apr 1831 – **Juan Antonio Gurule**, of this jurisdiction, widower of Maria Toribia Martin, deceased, m. **Maria Josefa Martin**, of this jurisdiction, legit d/ Jose Martin and Maria Rita Pando; pad/ Jose Santiago Garcia de la Mora and Maria Tomasa Martin, residents of Abiquiu; wit/ Domingo Martin and Jose Maria Trugillo. (pg 16/16b)

1 May 1831 – **Miguel Antonio Sena**, of this jurisdiction, widower of second nuptials, m. **Maria Elena Archuleta**, of this jurisdiction, d/ Dolores Archuleta; pad/ Juan Nepomuseno Baca and Guadalupe Baca, residents of Abiquiu; wit/ Jose Ysabel Maes and Jose Grabiel Gallego. (pg 16b)

2 May 1831 – **Miguel Antonio Marques**, of this jurisdiction, widower of Francisca Sisneros, deceased, m. **Maria Paubla Samora**, of this jurisdiction, widow of Jose Serrano, deceased; pad/ Pedro Jaramiyo and Maria Gertrudes Jaramiyo, residents of Abiquiu; wit/ Domingo Martin and Mariano Trugillo. (pg 16b/17)

22 May 1831 – **Ramon Antonio Espinosa**, of this jurisdiction, legit s/ Nicolas Espinosa and Maria Rita Vigil, m. **Maria Juana Guadalupe Archuleta**, of this jurisdiction, legit d/ Antonio Archuleta and Maria Moncerrate Leal; pad/ Juan Ysidro Gillen and Maria Ramona Gillen, residents of Abiquiu; wit/ Paublo Romero and Jose Ramon Manasares. (pg 17)

28 May 1831 – **Salbador Manuel Garcia**, of this jurisdiction, legit s/ Manuel Visente Garcia, deceased, and Maria Matilde Lusero, m. **Maria Barbara Martin**, of this jurisdiction, legit d/ Jose Martin, deceased, and Mariana Masquareñas; pad/ Francisco Valdes and Maria Jasinta Trugillo, residents of Abiquiu; wit/ Mariano Trugillo and Jose Santiago Trugillo. (pg 17/17b)

26 Jul 1831 – **Francisco Estevan Martin**, of this jurisdiction, legit s/ Juan Domingo Martin and Maria de Jesus Naranjo, m. **Maria Consepcion Segura**, of this jurisdiction, legit d/ Manuel Segura and Maria Rafaela Vigil; pad/ Rafael Baca and Maria Petra Bernal, residents of Abiquiu; wit/ Francisco Marques and Juan Agustin Chabes. (pg 17b)

26 Jul 1831 – **Diego Antonio Baldes**, of this jurisdiction, legit s/ Eusebio Baldes and Maria Dolores Gomes, m. **Juana Maria Gomes**, of this jurisdiction, legit d/ Juan Gomes and Maria de

la Lus Vigil, deceased; pad/ Pedro Gomes and Manuela Baldes, residents; wit/ Marcos Chabes and Juan Antonio Trugillo. (pg 17b / 18)

31 Jul 1831 – **Julian de la Jesus Trugillo**, of this jurisdiction, legit s/ Francisco Trugillo and Maria del Carmen Salas, m. **Juana Nepomusena Gallego**, of this jurisdiction, legit d/ Manuel Gallego and Maria de la Lus Martin; pad/ Juan Jose Olgin and Paubla Rodriges, residents of the Plaza of Santa Cruz of Ojo Caliente; wit/ Grabiel Maes and Ramon Cordoba. (pg 18)

9 Oct 1831 – **Vicente Lusero**, of this jurisdiction, legit s/ Manuel Lusero and Maria Casilda Maestas, m. **Maria Juliana Maes**, of this jurisdiction, legit d/ Salbador Maes and Manuela Garcia, deceased; pad/ Santos Lusero and Estefania Salasar, residents of Abiquiu; wit/ Pedro Atencio and Juan de Jesus Sisneros. (pg 18b)

11 Aug 1831 – **Santiago de Lao**, of this jurisdiction, legit s/ Jose de Lao and Anamaria Sena, m. **Maria Manuela Marques**, of this jurisdiction, legit d/ Manuel Marques and Maria Barbara Samora; pad/ Marcial Montolla and Rosalia Montolla, residents of Abiquiu; wit/ Jesus Maria Martin and Jose Apodaca. (pg 18b)

24 Oct 1831 – **Pedro Ygnacio Salasar**, of this jurisdiction, legit s/ Jose Manuel Salasar and Vibiana Sisneros, m. **Maria Asencion Vigil**, of this jurisdiction, legit d/ Jose Francisco Vigil, deceased, and Maria Dolores Lopes; pad/ Juan Vigil and Rafaela Sanches, residents of Santa Fe; wit/ Ramon Ruibal and Gregorio Atencio. (pg 19)

29 Oct 1831 – **Jose Mariano Mestas**, of this jurisdiction, legit s/ Jose Maria del Carmen Mestas and Maria Dolores Rodriges, m. **Maria Ygnacia Madrid**, of this jurisdiction, legit d/ Jose Antonio Madrid and Barbara Lusero; pad/ Sisto Martin, veciono of Abiquiu; wit/ Jose Maron Mansanares and Felipe Veita. (pg 19)

4 Nov 1831 – **Jose Vicente Gonsales**, of this jurisdiction, widower of second marriage, m. **Maria Guadalupe Jaramillo**, of this jurisdiction, d/ Rafaela Jaramillo; pad/ Rael Chaves and Ysabel Jaques, residents of Abiquiu; wit/ Juan Bautista Jaramillo and Juan Antonio Alire. (pg 19b)

18 Nov 1831 – **Ygnacio Atencio**, of this jurisdiction, legit s/ Miguel Atencio and Juana Manuela Martin, m. **Maria Candelaria Martin**, of this jurisdiction, legit d/ Antonio Martin, deceased, and Maria Gertrudis Salasar, deceased; pad/ Juan Atencio and Guadalupe Lusero, residents of Abiquiu; wit/ Thomas Salasar and Julian Ocaña. (pg 19b)

16 Nov 1831 – **Antonio de Jesus Martin**, of this jurisdiction, legit s/ Juan Pedro Martin, deceased, and Cerafina Trugillo, m. **Maria Rosalia Garcia**, of this jurisdiction, legit d/ Sisto

Garcia and Maria de los Reyes Lobato, deceased; pad/ Mariano Serrano and Maria Francisca Serrano, residents of Abiquiu; wit/ Domingo Martin and Jose de Jesus Olgin. (pg 20)

20 Nov 1831 – **Antonio de la Cruz Urtado**, of the Plaza of San Juan Nepomuseno, legit s/ Jasinto Urtado and Maria Francisca Quintana, m. **Maria Ramona Gillen**, of the Plaza of San Juan Nepomuseno, legit d/ Jose Manuel Gillen and Maria Cerafina de los Angeles Martin; pad/ Jose Antonio Martin and Dolores Urtado, residents of el Rito of San Juan Nepomuseno; wit/ Ramon Martin and Juan Simon Martin. (pg 20)

21 Nov 1831 – **Antonio Nerio Gomes**, of this jurisdiction, legit s/ Felipe Gomes, deceased, and Maria de la Luz Martin, m. **Maria Estefana Miera**, of this jurisdiction, legit d/ Antonio Miera and Catarina Sisneros; pad/ Jose Chaves and Dolores Martin, residents of Abiquiu; wit/ Manuel Marques and Domingo Abila. (pg 20b)

10 Dec 1831 – **Pedro Ygnacio Belasques**, of this jurisdiction, legit s/ Juan Antonio Belasques and Maria Ygnacia Chaves, m. **Maria Guadalupe Trugillo**, of this jurisdiction, d/ Maria Concepcion Trugillo; pad/ Juan Jose Baldes and Guadalupe Archuleta, residents of Abiquiu; wit/ Mariano Trugillo and Diego Madrid. (pg 20b)

13 Dec 1831 – **Jose Antonio Sebastian Muños**, of this jurisdiction, legit s/ Antonio Muños and Maria de la Lus Archuleta, m. **Maria Concepcion Trugillo**, of this jurisdiction, legit d/ Acencio Trugillo and Maria Micaela Lopes, deceased; pad/ Rafael Baca and Petra Bernal, residents of Abiquiu; wit/ Mariano Trugillo and Nicolas Lugan. (pg 21)

24 Dec 1831 – **Jose Francisco Baldes**, of this jurisdiction, widower of Maria Paubla Martin, deceased, m. **Maria Francisca Gallego**, of this jurisdiction, legit d/ Pedro Gallego and Maria Lorensa Espinosa; pad/ Pedro Trugillo and Maria Manuela Trugillo, residents of Abiquiu; wit/ Thomas Romero and Jose Santiago Trugillo. (pg 21)

27 Dec 1831 – **Felipe de Jesus Trugillo**, of this jurisdiction, legit s/ Paublin Trugillo, deceased, and Maria Josefa Martin, deceased, m. **Maria Soledad Barela**, of this jurisdiction, legit d/ Diego Barela and Maria de Lus Naranjo; pad/ Jose Antonio Martin and Consepcion Olgin, residents de Ojo Caliente; wit/ Jose Gallego and Baltasar Baca. (pg 21b)

7 Jan 1832 – **Francisco Estevan Garcia**, of this jurisdiction, legit s/ Juan Esteban Garcia and Maria Dolores Gutierres, deceased, m. **Maria de la Lus Chaves**, of this jurisdiction, legit d/ Juan Agustin Chaves and Maria Juana Martin; pad/ Pedro Trugillo and Maria Manuela Trugillo, residents of Abiquiu; wit/ Domingo Trugillo and Mariano Trugillo. (pg 21b)

No page 22

8 Jan 1832 – **Jose Pablo Beita**, of this jurisdiction, legit s/ Pablo Beita, deceased, and Anamaria Martin, deceased, m. **Maria Rosa de los Reyes Salasar**, of this jurisdiction, legit d/ Jose Manuel Salasar and Viviana Sisneros; pad/ Jose Antonio Martin and Maria de Jesus Villanueva, residents of Abiquiu; wit/ Esteban de Luna and Antonio de Jesus Martin. (pg 23)

14 Jan 1832 – **Jose Fernando Montaño**, of this jurisdiction, legit s/ Francisco Montaño and Margarita Martin, m. **Maria de Jesus Delgado**, of this jurisdiction, legit d/ Marcos Delgado and Guadalupe Baldes; pad/ Jose Maria del Socorro Ortiz and Guadalupe Alarid, residents of Abiquiu; wit/ Diego Belasques and Jose Albino Martin. (pg 23)

14 Jan 1832 – **Juan de Dios Moya**, of this jurisdiction, legit s/ Jose Moya and Maria Nicolasa Armijo, deceased, m. **Maria Consepcion Martin**, of this jurisdiction, d/ Patrocinia Martin; pad/ Juan Salasar and Maria Conscepcion Archuleta, residents of Abiquiu; wit/ Jose Pablo Trugillo and Fraoncisco Montaño. (pg 23b)

28 Jan 1832 – **Jose Cipriano Medina**, of this jurisdiction, legit s/ Diego Medina and Maria Francisca Gillen, m. **Maria Guadalupe Martin**, of this jurisdiction, d/ Maria Antonia Martin; pad/ Christobal Martin and Maria Josefa Alari, residents of Abiquiu; wit/ Candelario Ruibali and Cruz Baldes. (pg 23b)

16 Feb 1832 – **Manuel Martin**, of this jurisdiction, widower of 1st marriage to Maria Getrudes Martin, deceased, m. **Maria Andrea Garcia**, of this jurisdiction, legit d/ Jose Candelario Garcia and Maria Rita Archuleta; pad/ Juan de Jesus Lucero and Maria Getrudes Archuleta, residents of Abiquiu; wit/ Domingo Martin and Francisco Marques. (pg 24)

11 Mar 1832 – **Antonio Jose Mejicano**, of this jurisdiction, legit s/ Ysidro Mejicano and Francisca de Errera, m. **Maria de la Cruz Baldes**, of this jurisdiction, legit d/ Jose Manuel Baldes and Francisca Sisneros; pad/ Fernando Montaño and Maria de Jesus Delgado, residents of Abiquiu; wit/ Francisco Marques and Profiro Trugillo. (pg 24)

2 Apr 1832 – **Pasqual Bailon Archuleta**, of this jurisdiction, widower of 1st marriage to Antonia Visenta Naranjo, deceased, m. **Maria Serafina Salasar**, of this jurisdiction, legit d/ Juan Christobal Salasar, deceased, and Maria de la Cruz Varos; pad/ Jose Manuel Gillen and Serafina Martin, residents de San Juan Nepomuseno of el Rito; wit/ Manuel Atencio and Juan Jose Martin. (pg 24/24b)

12 Apr 1832 – **Juan Antonio Quintana**, of this jurisdiction, legit s/ Juan de Jesus Quintana and Maria Guadalupe Roival, m. **Maria Rafaela Martin**, of this jurisdiction, legit d/ Juan Manuel

Martin and Juana Catarina Baldes; pad/ Grabriel Baldes and Ana Maria Jaramillo, residents of Abiquiu; wit/ Juan Luna and Julian Madrid. (pg 24b)

29 Apr 1832 – **Jose Cisilio Atencio**, of this jurisdiction, legit s/ Julian Atencio and Maria Arntonia Varela, m. **Maria Bibiana Quintana**, of this jurisdiction, legit d/ Miguel Quintana and Maria Manuela Mondragon, deceased; pad/ Antonio Espinosa and Getrudes Archuleta, residents of Abiquiu; wit/ Antonio Gutierres and Bernardo Martin. (pg 24b)

11 Jul 1832 – **Jose de Jesus Garcia**, of this jurisdiction, legit s/ Rafael Garcia, deceased, and Maria Josefa Martin, deceased, m. **Maria Casimira Ramona Ruibal**, of this jurisdiction, legit d/ Thomas Ruibal and Josefa Espinosa; pad/ Juan Atencio and Guadalupe Lusero, residents of Abiquiu; wit/ Ysidro Martin and Jose Santiago Trugillo. (pg 25)

3 Sep 1832 – **Juan Christobal Lujan**, of this jurisdiction, legit s/ Salbador Lujan and Guadalupe Trujillo, deceased, m. **Maria Josefa Tageda**, of this jurisdiction, legit d/ Antonio Tageda and Paubla Vigil, deceased; pad/ Jose Pablo Beita and Maria Rosa de los Reyes Salasar, residents of Abiquiu; wit/ Felipe Garcia and Juan Antonio Trugillo. (pg 25)

20 Sep 1832 – **Juan Francisco Maestas**, of this jurisdiction, legit s/ Jose Antonio Maestas and Maria Manuela Trugillo, m. **Maria Antonia Martin**, of this jurisdiction, widow of Antonio Jose Garcia, deceased; pad/ Estevan Benabides and Dolores Benabides, residents of Abiquiu; wit/ Jose Rafael Duran and Thomas Chaves. (pg 25/25b)

23 Sep 1832 – **Juan Manuel Sanches**, of this jurisdiction, legit s/ Santiago Sanches, deceased, and Asencion Martin, m. **Juana Maria Gonsales**, of this jurisdiction, legit d/ Pasqual Gonsales and Balentia Trugillo; pad/ Diego Montoya and Maria de la Lus Montoya, residents of Abiquiu; wit/ Juan Antonio Gonsales and Pedro Jaramiyo. (pg 25b)

6 Oct 1832 – **Jose Miguel Trugillo**, of this jurisdiction, legit s/ Pedro Trugillo and Maria Antonia Sanches, m. **Maria Antonia Baldes**, of this jurisdiction, legit s/ Manuel Baldes and Maria Josefa Beita; pad/ Bernardo Muños and Barbara Montoya, residents of Abiquiu; wit/ Lorenzo Gallego and Rafael Baca. (pg 25b/26)

11 Oct 1832 – **Pedro Nolasco Mansanares**, of this jurisdiction, legit s/ Manuel Mansanares and Maria Asencion Sandoval, m. **Maria Ysabel Martin**, of this jurisdiction, legit d/ Pedro Martin, deceased, and Pasquala Trugillo; pad/ Juan de Jesus Lusero and Maria Getrudes Archuleta, residents of Abiquiu; wit/ Juan de Luna and Jose Santiago Trugillo. (pg 26)

1 Nov 1832 – **Jose Santiago Olivas**, of this jurisdiction, legit s/ Juan de Carmen Olivas and Maria de la Lus Vigil, m. **Maria Thomasa Madrid**, of this jurisdiction, legit d/ Christoval

Madrid and Maria Josefa Moya; pad/ Diego Madrid and Maria Manuela Jaramillo, residents of Abiquiu; wit/ Jose Rafael Duran and Nereo Naranjo. (pg 26)

1 Nov 1832 – **Jose Mariano Martin**, of this jurisdiction, legit s/ Manuel Gregorio Martin and Maria Paubla Martin, deceased, m. **Maria Manuela Lopes**, of this jurisdiction, legit d/ Pablo Lopes, deceased, and Rosalia Madrid, deceased; pad/ Francisco Trugillo and Maria de Jesus Trugillo, residents of Abiquiu; wit/ Juan Domingo Martin and Antonio Gutierres. (pg 26/26b)

6 Nov 1832 – **Juan Rafael Lopes**, of this jurisdiction, legit s/ Jose Ramon Lopes and Maria Lugarda Espinosa, m. **Maria Manuela Alarid**, of this jurisdiction, legit d/ Jose Manuel Aliri and Maria Dolores Maes; pad/ Juan Francisco Atencio and Guadalupe Lucero, residents of the Plaza of San Rafael; wit/ Julian Ocana and Miguel Gallego. (pg 26b)

9 Nov 1832 – **Jose Pablo Atencio**, of this jurisdiction, legit s/ Jose Manuel Atencio and Theodora Montoya, m. **Maria Dolores Martin**, of this jurisdiction, legit d/ Christobal Martin and Maria Josefa Alarid; pad/ Bernardo Muñis and Barbara Montoya, residents of Abiquiu; wit/ Thomas Martin and Victor Trugillo. (pg 26b)

21 Nov 1832 – **Jose de Jesus Lugan**, of this jurisdiction, legit s/ Nieves Lugan and Maria Soledad Romero, m. **Maria Manuela Trugillo**, of this jurisdiction, legit d/ Bartolo Trugillo, deceased, and Juana Angela Samora; pad/ Domingo Martin and Maria de la Cruz Gonsales, residents of Abiquiu; wit/ Mariano Trugillo and Jose Santiago Trugillo. (pg 27)

25 Nov 1832 – **Francisco Estevan Venavides**, of this jurisdiction, legit s/ Jose Antonio Venavides, deceased, and Maria Ramona Trugillo, m. **Maria de Jesus Martin**, of this jurisdiction, legit d/ Juan de Dios Martin, deceased, and Maria Antonia Garcia; pad/ Ramon Martin and Maria Manuela Gutierres, residents of Abiquiu; wit/ Ygnacio Trugillo and Felipe Garcia. (pg 27)

30 Nov 1832 – **Jose Antonio Mestas**, of this jurisdiction, legit s/ Luis Mestas and Maria Juana Archuleta, m. **Maria Juana Archuleta**, of this jurisdiction, legit d/ Marcial Archuleta and Maria del Carmen Gallego; pad/ Julian Trugillo and Juana Nepomuceno Gallego, residents of Santa Cruz of Ojo Caliente; wit/ Jose Rafael Duran and Juan Antonio Lusero. (pg 27/27b)

2 Dec 1832 – **Juan Prudencio Gonsales**, of this jurisdiction, legit s/ Juan Felipe Gonsales and Maria Guadalupe Toledo, m. **Maria Ygnacia Baldes**, of this jurisdiction, legit d/ Juan Baldes and Ana Maria Trugillo; pad/ Ramon Luna and Maria del Carmel Ortega, residents of Abiquiu; wit/ Jose Rafael Duran and Thomas Chaves. (pg 27b)

2 Dec 1832 – **Jose Felipe Santiago Lopes**, of this jurisdiction, legit s/ Juan Christoval Lopes and Manuela Chaves, deceased, m. **Maria Ysabel Martin**, of this jurisdiction, legit d/ Juan Simon Martin and Maria Josefa Serda; pad/ Crus Baldes and Manuela Salasar, residents of the plaza of San Juan Nepomuseno of el Rito; wit/ Juan Felipe Gonsales and Juan Andres Sanches. (pg 27b)

7 Dec 1832 – **Santiago Baldes**, of this jurisdiction, legit s/ Thomas Baldes, deceased, and Maria Pacifica Jacques, m. **Maria Sipriana Chacon**, of this jurisdiction, legit d/ Ygnacio Chacon, deceased, and Maria Pasquala Martin; pad/ Juan Simon Trugillo and Paula Torres, residents of the plaza of San Juan Nepomuseno of el Rito; wit/ Jose Rafael Duran and Juan Gutierres. (pg 27b/28)

8 Dec 1832 – **Jose Domingo Madrid**, of this jurisdiction, legit s/ Savaldor Madrid and Maria de la Lus Blea, m. **Maria de la Cruz Atencio**, of this jurisdiction, legit d/ Eilario Atencio and Maria Paubla Flores; pad/ Vicente Gonzales and Anamaria Jaramillo; wit/ Domingo Trugillo and Antonio Muños. (pg 28)

16 Dec 1832 – **Jose Francisco Trugillo**, of this jurisdiction, widower of 1st marriage to Maria Ygnacia Romero, m. **Maria Bibiana Martin**, of this jurisdiction, legit d/ Juan Martin and Maria Dolores Garcia; pad/ Cruz Baldes and Manuela de Salasar; wit/ Pablo Trujillo and Domingo Martin. (pg 28)

27 Dec 1832 – **Jose Manuel Delgado**, of the Plaza of San Rafael, legit s/ Marcos Delgado and Guadalupe Baldes, m. **Maria Paubla Baldes**, of the Plaza of San Rafael, legit d/ Julian Baldes and Maria Margarita Belarde; pad/ Rafael Ortiz and Maria Guadalupe Baca; wit/ Ramon Martin and Juan Agustin Chaves. (pg 29b)

29 Dec 1832 – **Juan Agustin Lucero**, of the Plaza of San Francisco, legit s/ Gregorio Lucero and Maria Telles, m. **Maria Soledad Salazar**, of the Plaza of San Francisco, legit d/ Manuel Salazar and Ana Maria Moya; pad/ Juan Salasar and Gregoria Archuleta; wit/ Esteban Venavides and Juan Jose Abila. (pg 29b)

page number 28b and 29a skipped

4 Jan 1833 – **Pedro Antonio Martin**, of the Plaza of San Juan Nepomuceno of el Rito, legit s/ Juan Martin and Maria Dolores Garcia, m. **Maria Ynes Trugillo**, of the Plaza of San Juan Nepomuceno of el Rito, legit d/ Antonio Trugillo and Maria Ygnacia Romero, deceased; pad/ Antonio Espinosa and Maria Jetrudes Archuleta, residents of the plaza of San Juan Nepomuceno of el Rito; wit/ Miguel Ruibali and Jesus Gonsales. (pg 29b/30)

13 Jan 1833 – **Jose Miguel Madrid**, of the Plaza of San Rafael, legit s/ Bernardo Madrid and Ysabel Lopes, m. **Maria Encarnacion Martin**, of the Plaza of San Rafael, legit d/ Antonio Martin, deceased, and Maria Getrudes Salasar; pad/ Jose Pablo Gallego and Maria Asencion Gallego, residents of the plaza of San Rafael; wit/ Profero Trugillo and Jose Miguel Jaramillo. (pg 30)

24 Jan 1833 – **Jose Antonio Alejandro Espinosa**, of el Rito, widower of 1st marriage to Encarnacion Lusero, deceased, m. **Maria Fabriana Gallego**, of el Rito, legit d/ Miguel Ascencio Gallego and Maria Guadalupe Rael; pad/ Manuel Atencio and Josefa Espinosa, residents of the plaza of San Juan Nepomuceno of el Rito; wit/ Mariano Trugillo and Domingo Trugillo. (pg 30/30b)

27 Jan 1833 – **Martin Romualdo Trugillo**, of the Plaza of San Juan Nepomuceno of el Rito, legit s/ Juan Francisco Trugillo and Maria del Carmen Salas, m. **Maria Juana Gomes**, of the Plaza of San Juan Nepomuceno of el Rito, legit d/ Mariano Mateo Gomes and Silveria Martin; pad/ Juan Francisco Gutierres and Maria Candelaria Martin, residents de San Fernando; wit/ Juan Benito Sanches and Rafael Gonsales. (pg 30b)

20 Feb 1833 – **Juan de Jesus Herrera**, of the Plaza of Nuestra Señora de Guadalupe, legit s/ Crus Herrera and Maria Getrudis Salasar, m. **Maria Rufina Baldes**, of the Plaza of Nuestra Señora of Guadalupe, legit d/ Tomas Baldes, deceased and Pasifica Jaques; pad/ Seledon Herrera and Guadalupe Baca, residents of Abiquiu; wit/ Jose Ysabel Maes and Francisco Martin. (pg 30b)

2 Mar 1833 – **Jose Maria Martin**, of Abiquiu, legit s/ Jose Martin and Maria Dolores Archuleta, m. **Maria Miquela Baldes**, of Abiquiu, legit d/ Rafael Baldes, deceased and Maria Antonia Baca; pad/ Jose Manuel Jaramillo and Maria Manuela Chacon, residents de Santo Tomas of Abiquiu; wit/ Rafael Luxan and Jose Antonio Quintana. (pg 31)

10 Mar 1833 – **Matias Chaves**, of Abiquiu, legit s/ Juan Jose Chaves and Maria de Jesus Serda, m. **Maria Cristesna Montoya**, of Abiquiu, legit d/ Manuel Montoya and Polonia Bernal; pad/ Jose Chaves and Estefana Lucero, residents of Abiquiu; wit/ Miguel Garcia and Jose Rafael Duran. (pg 31)

26 Mar 1833 – **Manuel Gutierres**, of Abiquiu, widower, m. **Maria Dolores Benabides**, of Abiquiu, legit d/ Jose Antonio Benabides, deceased, and Ramona Trugillo; pad/ Rafael Baca and Guadalupe Baca, residents of Abiquiu; wit/ Ramon Lopes and Rafael Trugillo. (pg 31b)

15 Apr 1833 – **Juan Francisco Atencio**, of the Plaza de Nuestra Señora de Guadalupe, legit s/ Miguel Atencio and Manuela Martin, m. **Maria Josefa Jaques**, of the Plaza de Nuestra Señora

de Guadalupe, legit d/ Felipe Jaques and Maria del Carmen Lugan; pad/ Felipe Jaques and Micaela Torres, of the Plaza de Nuestra Señora de Guadalupe; wit/ Mariano Trugillo and Lorenso Trugillo. (pg 31b)

19 Apr 1833 – **Thomas de Aquino Archuleta**, of the Plaza of San Miguel, legit s/ Juan Antonio Archuleta and Juana Martin, m. **Maria Josefa Molina**, of the Plaza of San Miguel, widow of Nicolas Garcia; pad/ Juan Beita and Maria Manuela Baca, residents of the plaza of San Miguel; wit/ Pasqual Gonsales and Nicolas Trugillo. (pg 32)

Nota, m. (pg 32/32b)

20 Aug 1833 – **Pantalion Archuleta**, legit s/ Juan Andres Archuleta and Margarita Lusero, m. **Maria Rafaela Agilar**, legit d/ Jose Antonio Agilar and Maria de la Lus Quintana; pad/ Juan Olgin and Maria Paubla Rodriges, residents of the plaza of Santa Cruz; wit/ Jose Belasques and Jose Antonio Martin. (pg 32b)

10 Oct 1833 – **Felipe Antonio Lovato**, widower in the 1st marriage to Maria Miquela Marques, m. **Maria Dolores Chacon**, of Ojo Caliente, legit d/ Ygnacio Chacon, deceased, and Maria Pasquala Martin, deceased, from Ojo Caliente. (pg 32b)

2[torn] 1833 – **Juan Faustin Chacon**, of Abiquiu, single legit s/ Ygnacio Chacon and Pascuala Martin, m. **Andrea Valdes** d/ Tomas Valdes, deceased, and Maria Pacifica Jaques; wit/ Juan de Jesus Ruibali and Jose Pablo Medina. (pg 33)

25 Nov 1833 – **Jose Vicente Marques**, of this jurisdiction, single s/ Diego Marques and Ygnacia Gallego, m. **Maria Gertrudes Chacon**, of this jurisdiction, d/ Ygnacio Chacon, deceased, and Pascuala Martin, deceased; wit/ Juan Gutierrez and Salbador Gonsales. (pg 33)

25 Nov 1833 – **Jose Gabriel Baldes**, of this jurisdiction, s/ Bernardo Baldes and Ana Maria Jaramillo, m. **Maria Barbara Martin** d/ Ygnacio Martin and Maria Josefa Trugillo; wit/ Jose Rafael Duran, Martin Romualdo Trugillo. (pg 33/33b)

27 Nov 1833 – **Juan de Jesus Gomes**, of this jurisdiction, s/ Gaspar Gomes and Maria Mez, m. **Maria Guadalupe Martin** d/ Antonio Martin and Maria Ygnacia Valdes; wit/ Jose Pablo Archuleta and Juan Ygnacio Ortega. (next page, torn)

16 Dec 1833 – **Juan Antonio Martin**, s/ Pedro Antonio Martin and Maria Teodora Gonsales, m. **Maria Salome Velasques**, of this jurisdiction, d/ Joaquin Velasques and Maria Antonia Romero; wit/ (torn) Marcos Delgado and Juan (torn). (next page, torn)

6 Dec 1833 – **Profero Trugillo**, of this jurisdiction, widower, m. **Maria Josefa Garcia**, of this jurisdiction, d/ Felipe Santiago Garcia and Maria Rosalia Mestas; wit/ Jose Pablo Archuleta and Juan Ygnacio Ortega. (next page, torn)

26 Dec 1833 – **Juan Antonio Gallego**, of this jurisdiction, s/ Domingo Gallego and Maria Barbara Espinosa, m. **Maria Trinidad Olguin**, of this jurisdiction, d/ Cristobal Olguin and Maria Josefa Velasques; wit/ Jose Rafael Duran and Acencio Trugillo. (next page, torn)

27 Dec 1833 – **Antonio Rafael Archuleta**, of this jurisdiction, widower, m. **Maria Manuela Medina**, of this jurisdiction, d/ Gregorio Medina and Maria Ysabel Romero; wit/ Jose Eucebio Valdes and Jose de la Cruz Gonsales. (next page, torn)

11 Jan 1834 – **Mariano Peña**, of this jurisdiction, s/ Manuel Peña and Maria Vitalia Maes, deceased, m. **Maria Guadalupe Trugillo**, of this jurisdiction, d/ Juan Trugillo and Maria Josefa Roibal; wit/ Jose Manuel Martines and Jose Ramon Valdes. (next page, torn)

30 Jan 1834 – **Jose Cristobal Garcia** m. **Maria Bibiana Martin**. (incomplete and not on next page)

12 Nov 1834 – **Jose Ramon Blas Garcia**, of this jurisdiction, s/ Juan Antonio Garcia and Manuela Trugillo, m. **Maria de la Crus Valdes**, of this jurisdiction, d/ Jose Francisco Valdes, deceased, and Maria Ygnacia Chabes, deceased; wit/ Pablo Lucero and Salvador Sanches. (pg 39)

16 Nov 1834 – **Juan Bautista Lopes**, of this jurisdiction, s/ Ramon Lopes and Maria Lugarda Espinosa, m. **Maria del Refugio Jaramillo**, of this jurisdiction, d/ Patricio Jaramillo and Francisca Olguin, deceased; wit/ Jose Rafael Duran, Jose Miguel Jaramillo and Jose Santiago Velasques. (pg 39)

25 Nov 1834 – **Francisco Antonio Olguin**, of this jurisdiction, s/ Cristobal Olguin, deceased, and Maria Josefa Velasques, m. **Ana Maria Vigil**, of this jurisdiction, d/ Faustin Vigil, deceased, and Maria Manuela Jaramillo; wit/ Juan Agustin Chabes and Jose Hipolito Jaramillo. (pg 39b)

27 Nov 1834 – **Jose Ramon Garcia**, of this jurisdiction, s/ Juan Luis Garcia and Reyes Lobato, m. **Maria de Jesus Ortega**, of this jurisdiction, d/ Jose Antonio Ortega and Antonia Rosa Valdes; wit/ Jose Miguel Gonsales, Juan Antonio Velasques and Manuel Garcia. (pg 39b)

28 Nov 1834 – **Jose Antonio Lopes**, of this jurisdiction, s/ Miguel Lopes and Maria Josefa Martin, deceased, m. **Maria Encarnacion Lucero**, of this jurisdiction, d/ Pablo Lucero and

Maria Gertrudes Salas, deceased; wit/ Juan Agustin Chabes and Jose Antonio Salasar. (pg 39b/40)

7 Dec 1834 – **Jose de la Crus Gonsales** m. **Maria Ana Trugillo,** widow of this jurisdiction; wit/ Mariano Trugillo, Antonio Gutierres and Juan Jose Abila. (pg 40)

14 Dec 1834 – **Juan Jose Espinosa**, of this jurisdiction, s/ Juan Pedro Espinosa, deceased, and Maria Juana Valdes, m. **Maria de la Lus Salasar**, of this jurisdiction, d/ Jose Miguel Salasar and Maria Manuela de Errera; wit/ Juan Ribera and Antonio Vigil. (pg 40/40b)

28 Dec 1834 – **Jose Manuel Vigil**, of this jurisdiction, s/ Jose Manuel Vigil, deceased, and Estefana Martin, m. **Maria de Esquipula Quintana**, of this jurisdiction, d/ Agustin Quintana and Maria Dolores Lucero; wit/ D. Salvador Lucero, D. Jose Antonio Martin and D. Jose Antonio Aguilar. (pg 40b)

29 Dec 1834 – **Pedro Acencio Valdes**, of this jurisdiction, s/ Usebio Valdes and Maria Dolores Chaves, m. **Ana Maria de los Dolores Vigil**, of this jurisdiction, d/ Juan de Jesus Vigil and Maria Manuela Martin, deceased; wit/ Hipolito Trugillo and Felipe de Jesus Trugillo. (pg 40b/41)

29 Dec 1834 – **Juan Antonio Trugillo**, of this jurisdiction, s/ Rafael Trugillo and Martina Garcia, m. **Maria Candelaria Lujan**, of this jurisdiction, d/ Pedro Leon Lujan and Maria Manuela Garcia; wit/ Jose Martin and Jose Gonsales. (pg 41)

29 Dec 1834 – **Juan de Esquipula Velasquez**, of this jurisdiction, s/ Joaquin Velasquez and Antonia Rosa Romero, m. **Maria Rita Garcia**, of this jurisdiction, d/ Sisto Garcia and Maria de los Reyes Lobato, deceased; wit/ Ramon Gallego, Miguel Antonio Romero and Felis Jaramillo. (pg 41/41b)

1 Jan 1835 – **Jose Maria Valdes**, of this jurisdiction, s/ Juan Pedro Valdes and Ana Maria Espinosa, m. **Maria Manuela Atencio**, of this jurisdiction, d/ Jose Manuel Atencio and Maria Teodora Montoya; wit/ Martin de Jesus Martin and Juan Domingo Martin. (pg 41b)

4 Jan 1835 – **Jose Justo Atencio**, of this jurisdiction, s/ Pedro Antonio Atencio and Maria Francisca Nieto, deceased, m. **Maria Francisca Lucero**, of this jurisdiction, d/ Ramon Lucero and Paula Duran; wit/ Nicolas Trugillo and Juan Agustin Chabes. (pg 41b/42)

14 Jan 1835 – **Jose Benito Martin**, of this jurisdiction, s/ Pablo Martin and Maria Concepcion Romero, m. **Maria Agueda Noriega**, of this jurisdiction, d/ Jose Noriega, deceased, and Maria Juana Ramires; wit/ Jesus Maria Varela and Juan Manuel Atencio. (pg 42)

21 Jan 1835 – **Jose Maria Martin**, of this jurisdiction, s/ Antonio Martin and Maria Manuela Gutierrez, m. **Juana Rosalia Lucero**, of this jurisdiction, d/ Gregorio Lucero and Martina Trugillo; wit/ Ramon Lucero and Jose Miguel Romero. (pg 42)

21 Jan 1835 – **Jose Santiago Martin**, of this jurisdiction, s/ Tomas Martin and Petrona Romero, m. **Maria de Jesus Chabes**, of this jurisdiction, d/ Juan Miguel Chabes, deceased, and Guadalupe Ortis; wit/ Eucebio Chabes and Jose Gabriel Sisneros. (pg 42b)

25 Jan 1835 – **Jesus Maria Martin**, of this jurisdiction, s/ Rafael Martin, deceased, and Maria de la Lus Sisneros, m. **Maria Josefa Lucero**, of this jurisdiction, d/ Miguel Lucero, deceased, and Maria de la Lus Martin, deceased; wit/ Juan Gutierres, Jose de Jesus Olguin and Rafael Baca. (pg 42b)

30 Apr 1835 – **Jose Guadalupe Quintana**, of this jurisdiction, s/ Jesus Quintana and Maria Guadalupe Roibal, m. **Maria Juliana Gracia Martin**, of this jurisdiction, d/ Cristobal Martin and Maria Josefa Alarid; wit/ Joaquin Velasques, Rafael Trugillo and Juan Agustin Chabes. (pg 42b/43)

1 May 1835 – **Jose Maria Lucero**, of this jurisdiction, s/ Miguel Lucero, deceased, and Maria de la Lus Martin, m. **Maria Luisa Valdes**, of this jurisdiction, d/ Jose Ramon Valdes and Maria de Jesus Chabes, deceased; wit/ Diego de Luna and Juan Agustin Chabes. (pg 43)

15 May 1835 – **Jose Vicente Faustin Velarde**, of this jurisdiction, s/ Jose Miguel Velarde and Maria Concepcion Duran, m. **Maria de Jesus Salazar**, of this jurisdiction, d/ Francisco Antonio Salazar, deceased, and Maria Manuela Gallego; wit/ Pedro Leon Lujan, Jose Martin and Miguel Antonio Garcia. (pg 43/43b)

19 May 1835 – **Antonio Domingo Lucero**, of this jurisdiction, s/ Julian Lucero and Barbara Sisneros, m. **Maria Rufina Valdes**, of this jurisdiction, d/ Bernardo Valdes and Ana Maria Jaramillo; wit/ Jose Martin and Miguel Antonio Garcia. (pg 43b)

28 Jun 1835 – **Juan Bautista Gallego**, of this jurisdiction, s/ Miguel Acencio Gallego and Maria Guadalupe Rael, m. **Maria Luisa Guillen**, of this jurisdiction, d/ Jose Manuel Guillen and Serafina Martin; wit/ Jose Rafael Duran and Tomas Roibal. (pg 43b)

25 Jul 1835 – **Juan Luis del Refugio Roibal**, of this jurisdiction, s/ Tomas Roibal and Josefa Espinosa, m. **Maria Trinidad Trugillo**, of this jurisdiction, d/ Francisco Trugillo and Maria Ygnacia Romero; wit/ Francisco Marques and Domingo Martin. (pg 44)

13 Sep 1835 – **Jose Antonio Martin**, of this jurisdiction, s/ Manuel Martin and Maria Manuela Quintana, m. **Maria Andrea Garcia**, of this jurisdiction, d/ Antonio Garcia and Maria Luisa Lucero; wit/ Juan Cristobal Valdes and Baltasar Quintana. (pg 44)

27 Sep 1835 – **Antonio Jose Serda**, of this jurisdiction, widower, m. **Maria del Carmen Gomes**, widow; wit/ Rafael Duran and Matias Jaramillo. (pg 44/44b)

<u>24</u> Oct 1835 – **Mariano Garcia**, of this jurisdiction, s/ Felipe Garcia and Maria del Rosario Mestas, m. **Maria de la Luz Chabes**, of this jurisdiction, d/ Antonio Jose Chabez, deceased, and Maria de la Acencion Martin; wit/ Domingo Trugillo and Ramon Martin. (pg 44b)

23 Oct 1835 – **Antonio Andres Lujan**, of this jurisdiction, s/ Manuel Lujan and Antonia Josefa Trugillo, m. **Maria Guadalupe Jaramillo**, of this jurisdiction, d/ Juan Manuel Jaramillo and Feliciana Valdes; wit/ Bernardo Sanches and Profeso Trugillo. (pg 44b)

25 Oct 1835 – **Jose Gabriel Espinosa**, of this jurisdiction, s/ Jose Antonio Espinosa, deceased, and Maria Tomasa Martin, deceased, m. **Maria Estefana Valdes**, of this jurisdiction, d/ Ramon Valdes, deceased, and Maria Pacifica Jaques; wit/ D. Juan Jose Olguin and D. Manuel Lorenzo Martin. (pg 45)

25 Oct 1835 – **Jose Manuel Mansanares**, of this jurisdiction, s/ Manuel Mansanares and Maria Acencion Martin, m. **Maria Simona Cordoba**, of this jurisdiction, d/ Juan de Jesus Cordoba and Juana Maria Garcia; wit/ Juan Cristobal Trugillo and Jose Pedro Gomes. (pg 45)

24 Oct 1835 – **Miguel Atencio**, of this jurisdiction, s/ Julian Atencio, deceased, and Antonia Barela, m. **Maria Rafaela Martin**, of this jurisdiction, d/ Antonio Martin and Maria Gertrudes Salasar, deceased; wit/ Miguel Antonio Gallego and Antonio Vigil. (pg 45/45b)

24 Oct 1835 – **Antonio Romaldo Jaramillo**, of this jurisdiction, s/ Patricio Jaramillo and Francisca Olgin, deceased, m. **Maria Ascencion Chaves**, of this jurisdiction, d/ Juan Bernardo Chaves and Maria de la Lus Archuleta; wit/ Jose Encarnacion Cacillas and Jose Gregorio Atencio. (pg 45b)

24 Oct 1835 – **Juan Jose Castillo**, of this jurisdiction, s/ Juan Jose Castillo, deceased, and Maria Rosa Espinosa, m. **Faustina Martin**, of this jurisdiction, d/ Ramon Martin and Romualda Atencio; wit/ Bentura Atencio and Jose Miguel Gonsales. (pg 45b/46)

6 Nov 1835 – **Ramon Manchego**, of this jurisdiction, s/ Jose Manuel Manchego and Maria de la Crus Ortis, m. **Ana Maria de los Dolores Ruibali**, of this jurisdiction, d/ Juan Antonio Ruibali, deceased, and Maria Gertrudes Gallego; wit/ Juan Atencio and Miguel Gonsales. (pg 46)

6 Nov 1835 – **Juan de Dios Lucero**, of this jurisdiction, s/ Ramon Lucero and Maria Paula Duran, deceased, m. **Maria Dolores Archuleta**, of this jurisdiction, d/ Manuel de Jesus Archuleta and Maria Gertrudes Trugillo; wit/ Diego Antonio Gomes, Jose Atencio and others of this church. (pg 46)

7 Nov 1835 – **Jose Rafael Alire**, of this jurisdiction, s/ Jose Manuel Alire and Maria Dolores Maes, m. **Maria Dolores Trugillo**, of this jurisdiction, d/ Juan de Dios Trugillo and Maria Antonia Mestas; wit/ Manuel Gallego, Pablo Romero and others. (pg 46b)

18 Nov 1835 – **Jose Tomas Chacon**, of this parish, s/ Noberto Chacon, deceased, and Maria Gertrudes Moya, m. **Maria Feliciana Archuleta**, of this same jurisdiction, d/ Nicolas Archuleta and Maria Candelaria Martin; wit/ Manuel Gallego, Jose de Jesus Olguin and others. (pg 46b)

18 Nov 1835 – **Cristobal Montoya**, of this parish, widower, m. **Maria Manuela Gonsales**, of this same jurisdiction, d/ Juan Cristobal Gonsalcs and Maria Candclaria Garcia; wit/ Carlos Torres, Santiago Velasques and others. (pg 46b/47)

29 Nov 1835 – **Francisco Antonio Martin**, widower of this parish, m. **Maria Dolores Martin**, of this same jurisdiction, d/ Pablo Martin and Maria Gertrudes Lopez, deceased; wit/ Jose Manuel Jaramillo, Pedro Valdes, Roque Sanches and others. (pg 47)

29 Nov 1835 – **Jose Francisco Rivera**, single of this parish, s/ Juan de Dios Rivera and Maria Cararima Montoya, m. **Maria Perfecta Mestas**, of this same jurisdiction, d/ Luis Mestas and Maria del Carmen Gallego; wit/ Jose Manuel Jaramillo, Pedro Valdes and others. (pg 47)

6 Dec 1835 – **Jose Miguel <u>Chacon</u>**, of this parish, s/ Agustin <u>Chabes</u> and Juana Martin, m. **Maria Estefana Gutierres**, of this same jurisdiction, d/ Juan Gutierres and Guadalupe Martin; wit/ Ygnacio Trugillo, Ramon Martin and others. (pg 47b)

6 Dec 1835 – **Jose Antonio Chabes**, of this parish, s/ Juan Agustin Chabes and Maria Juana Martin, m. **Juana Rosalia Garcia**, of this same jurisdiction, d/ Jose Maria Garcia and Maria Manuela Coris; wit/ Domingo Trugillo, Ramon Martin and others. (pg 47b)

11 Dec 1835 – **Antonio Romaldo <u>Ruibali</u>**, of this parish, s/ Gregorio <u>Urribali</u> and Josefa Mansanares, m. **Cararina del Refugio Sanches**, of this same jurisdiction, d/ Antonio Sanches, deceased, and Viviana de Luna; wit/ Salvador Gonsales, Jose Martin and others. (pg 47b/48)

18 Dec 1835 – **Jose Ygnacio Romero**, of this parish, s/ Juan Francisco Romero and Maria Nasarena Salazar, m. **Maria Rosa Martin**, of this same jurisdiction, d/ Patricia Martin; wit/ Noberto Naranjo, Francisco Antonio Olguin and others. (pg 48)

25 Dec 1835 – **Juan Cristobal Lujan**, of this parish, s/ Nicolas Lujan and Maria Soledad Romero, m. **Juana Molina**, of this same jurisdiction, d/ Lorenso Molina and Maria Josefa Trugillo, deceased; wit/ Mariano Trugillo, Rafael Trugillo, Juan Jose Martin and others. (pg 48/48b)

25 Dec 1835 – **Manuel de Esquipula Salasar**, of this parish, s/ Maria de Las Ascencion Salasar, m. **Maria Francisca Serrano**, of this same jurisdiction, d/ Ypolito Serrano and Maria Manuela Mestas; wit/ Juan Griego, Juan [illegible], Miguel Antonio Romero and others. (pg 48b)

28 Dec 1835 – **Francisco Estevan Trugillo**, of this parish, s/ Nicolas Trugillo and Maria Barbara Martin, deceased, m. **Maria de la Lus Jaramillo**, of this same jurisdiction, d/ Juan Agustin Jaramillo, deceased, and Maria de los Reyes Valdes; wit/ Domingo Trugillo, Ramon Martin and others. (pg 48b/49)

3 Jan 1836 – **Diego Antonio Serda**, of this parish, s/ Domingo Serda and Maria Manuela Martin, m. **Maria Josefa Gomes**, of this same jurisdiction, d/ Jose Miguel Segura and Maria Soledad Gomes; wit/ Francisco Moñtano, Ramon Romero and others. (pg 49)
start
3 Jan 1836 – **Jose Maria Valdes**, of this parish, s/ Manuel Valdes and Maria Josefa Beita, m. **Maria Juana Castelo**, of this same jurisdiction, d/ Mariano Castelo, deceased, and Maria Yisdora Ortega; wit/ Cristoval Manchego, Mariano Alarid, Julian Madrid and others. (pg 49/49b)

6 Jan 1836 – **Jose Ygnacio Salasar**, of this parish, s/ Santiago Salasar and Maria Dolores Romero, m. **Maria Juliana Gracia Montoya**, of this same jurisdiction, d/ Jose Manuel Montoya and Maria Loreta Pacheco; wit/ Pedro Trugillo, Nicolas Trugillo and others. (pg 49b)

6 Jan 1836 – **Mariano Serrano**, of this parish, s/ Ypolito Serrano and Maria Manuela Mestas, m. **Maria Dolores Beita**, of this same jurisdiction, d/ Juan Nepomuceno Beita and Maria Manuela Castelo; wit/ Eugenio Naranjo, Cristobal Martin and others. (pg 49b/50)

23 Jan 1836 – **Felipe Santiago Peña**, of this parish, s/ Pedro Peña and Maria del Carmen Jiron, m. **Maria Dolores Mestas**, of this same jurisdiction, d/ Feliciano Mestas, deceased, and Maria Madalena Vigil; wit/ Vicente Lucero, Ramon Lucero and others. (pg 50)

14 Feb 1836 – **Felipe de Jesus de Errera**, widower, m. **Maria Dolores Benabides,** all residents of this jurisdiction, widow; wit/ Salvador Lujan, Juan Gutierres and others. (pg 50/50b)

20 Apr 1836 – **Juan Antonio Gallego**, of this parish, s/ Domingo Gallego and Maria Barbara Espinosa, deceased, m. **Maria Trinidad Olguin**, of this same jurisdiction, d/ Cristobal Olguin, deceased, and Maria Josefa Velasquez; wit/ Salvador Lujan, Juan Gutierres and others. (pg 50b)

30 Apr 1836 – **Jesus Maria Garcia**, of this parish, s/ Jose Antonio Garcia and Maria Felipa Mondragon, m. **Maria Agreda Gallego**, of this same jurisdiction, d/ Jose Gallego and Maria Manuela Ruibali; wit/ Francisco Martin, Miguel Alari and others. (pg 50b/51)

1 May 1836 – **Manuel Antonio Gallego**, of this parish, s/ Rafael Gallego and Maria Antonia Lucero, deceased, m. **Maria Bibiana Gonsales**, of this same jurisdiction, widow; wit/ Jose Marcos Montoya, Juan de los Reyes Salasar and others. (pg 51)

15 Jun 1836 – **Jose Maria Martin**, of this parish, s/ Antonio Martin and Polonia Quintana, deceased, m. **Maria de la Lus Salasar**, of this same jurisdiction, d/ Manuel Salasar and Juana Josefa Valdes; wit/ Antonio Garcia, Juan de Dios Trugillo and others. (pg 51)

23 Jun 1836 – **Pedro Antonio Jaramillo**, of this parish, s/ Jose Antonio Jaramillo, deceased, and Rafaela Samora, m. **Maria Ygnes Madrid**, of this same jurisdiction, d/ Salvador Madrid, deceased, and Maria Elena Martin; wit/ Santiago Gonsales, Tomas Roibal and others. (pg 51b)

4 Sep 1836 – **Felipe Martin**, of this parish, s/ Dolores Trugillo, m. **Maria Ramona Errera**, of this same jurisdiction, d/ Felipe de Errera and Maria Rita Bustos; wit/ Jose Martin, Noberto Naranjo and others. (pg 51b)

4 Sep 1836 – **Pedro Antonio Martin**, of this parish, s/ Juan de Dios Martin, deceased, and Maria de Jesus Salasar, m. **Maria Ygnacia de Errera**, of this same jurisdiction, d/ Felipe de Herrera and Maria Rita Bustos; wit/ Jose Rafael Duran, Jose Pablo Trugillo and others. (pg 51b/52)

28 Oct 1836 – **Manuel Gregorio Gallego**, of this parish, s/ Diego Gallego and Maria Antonia Quintana, m. **Juana Romero**, of this same jurisdiction, d/ Santos Romero and Maria Antonia Encarnacion Maes; wit/ Cristobal Trugillo, Marcos Montoya and others. (pg 52)

31 Oct 1836 – **Juan Pablo Antonio Montoya**, of this parish, s/ Juan Vicente Montoya and Maria Dolores Urtado, m. **Maria Tomasa Gonsales**, of this same jurisdiction, d/ Pablo Gonsales, deceased, and Maria Paula Atencio; wit/ Jose Martin, Noberto Naranjo and others. (pg 52/52b)

26 Nov 1836 – **Jose Maria Velasques**, of this parish, s/ Joaquin Velasques and Antonia Rosa Romero, deceased, m. **Maria Concepcion Gallego**, of this same jurisdiction, d/ Julian Gallego and Josefa Montoya; wit/ Miguel Antonio Romero, Jose de Jesus Olguin and others. (pg 52b)

26 Nov 1836 – **Policarpio Martin Lucero**, single of this parish, s/ Cristobal Lucero and Maria Josefa Naranjo, deceased, m. **Maria Dolores Ruibali**, of this same jurisdiction, d/ Ramon Ruibali, deceased, and Maria Josefa Lucero; wit/ Manuel Apodaca, Juan Velasques and others. (pg 52b/53)

3 Dec 1836 – **Jose Dolores Gonsales,** single of this parish, s/ Jose Antonio Gonsales and Maria de la Lus Balverde, m. **Maria de la Lus Martin**, of this same jurisdiction, d/ Joaquin Martin and Maria Rosalia Valdes; wit/ Nicolas Martin, Jesus Maria Garcia and others. (pg 53)

10 Dec 1836 – **Juan Gabriel Chacon**, of this parish, s/ Amado Ygnacio Chacon and Pasquala Martin, m. **Maria de la Lus Vasques**, of this same jurisdiction, d/ Jose Velasques and Maria Estefana Martin; wit/ Rafael Gallego, Francisco Trugillo and others. (pg 53/53b)

12 Dec 1836 – **Juan Prudencio Gonsales**, of this parish, widower, m. **Juana Maria Archuleta**, of this same jurisdiction, d/ Antonio Aban Archuleta and Maria Antonia Rivera; wit/ Antonio Prieto, Jose Manuel Martin and others. (pg 53b)

28 Jan 1837 – **Juan de Jesus Truxillo**, of this parish, s/ Pedro Truxillo and Maria Antonia Sanches, m. **Maria Josefa Montaño**, of this same jurisdiction, d/ Faustino Montaño and Maria Encarnacion Velarde; wit/ Pedro Leon Lujan, Mariano Truxillo and others. (pg 53b/54)

28 Jan 1837 – **Nasario Truxillo**, of this parish, s/ Leon Truxillo and Maria Antonia Sanches, m. **Maria Juana Lucero**, of this same jurisdiction, d/ Miguel Lucero, deceased, and Maria de la Luz Martin; wit/ Mariano Truxillo, Rafael Jaramillo and others. (pg 54)

28 Jan 1837 – **Jose Francisco Salasar**, of this parish, s/ Francisco Antonio Salasar, deceased, and Maria Manuela Gallego, m. **Maria Biviana Garcia**, of this same jurisdiction, d/ Pablo Garcia and Maria Gertrudes Beitia; wit/ Pedro Leon Lujan, Jose Pablo Truxillo and others. (pg 54/54b)

28 Jan 1837 – **Jose Gabriel Valdes**, of this parish, s/ Rafael Valdes and Maria Antonia Baros, m. **Maria de la Lus Ruibali**, of this same jurisdiction, d/ Ramon Ruibali and Maria Loreta Lucero; wit/ Pedro Sandoval, Jose Ramon Martin and others. (pg 54b)

16 Feb 1837 – **Manuel Antonio Martin**, of this parish, adopted s/ German Valdes and Josefa Gomes, m. **Ana Maria Mansanares**, of this same jurisdiction, d/ Manuel Antonio Mansanares and Maria Ascencion Martin; wit/ Juan de Dios Trugillo, Roman Sisneros and others. (pg 54b)

18 Feb 1837 – **Jose Maria Santiago Truxillo**, of this parish, s/ Jose Juan Truxillo, deceased, and Maria Luiza Gallego, m. **Maria Guadalupe Jacques**, of this same jurisdiction, d/ Felipe Jacques and Maria del Carmel Lujan; wit/ Juan Nepomuceno Truxillo, Salvador Lucero and others. (pg 55)

18 Feb 1837 – **Juan de Jesus Herrera**, of this parish, s/ Jose Herrera and Maria Luzia Medina, m. **Maria Gertrudes Trugillo**, of this same jurisdiction, d/ father unknown and with the consent of the mother; wit/ Santiago Martin, Jose Ygnacio Trugillo and others. (pg 55)

22 Feb 1837 – **Juan Ramon Truxillo**, of this parish, s/ Mariano Truxillo and Bernanda Truxillo, m. **Maria Romualda Archuleta**, of this same jurisdiction, d/ Jose Archuleta and Maria Manuela Olguin; wit/ Pedro Leon Lujan, Miguel Garcia and others. (pg 55/55b)

26 Feb 1837 – **Antonio Jose Martines**, of this parish, s/ Juan Jose Martines and Maria Josefa Villalpando, m. **Maria Josefa Barela**, widow of Juan Manuel Copa, d/ Cristobal Barela, deceased, and Maria Rafaela Martin; wit/ Jose Manuel Valdes, Jose Manuel Salazar and others. (pg 55b)

21 Mar 1837 – **Benito Vigil**, of this parish, s/ Faustin Vigil and Maria de la Lus Martin, m. **Maria Gertrudes Gallego**, of this same jurisdiction, d/ Julian Gallego and Maria Josefa Montoya; wit/ Pedro Leon Lujan, Profero Trugillo and others. (pg 55b)

Abiquiu, New Mexico ~ Marriages
21 Nov 1845 – 16 Oct 1853

Priest notation.

21 Nov 1845 – **Miguel Antonio Gallego**, legit s/ Manuel Gallego and Maria de la Lus Martines, residents of Rito, m. **Maria Paubla Trujillo**, resident of same place, legit d/ Acension Trujillo and Soledad Muños; pad/ Jose Damian Jiron and Maria Ygnacia Martin, of el Rito; wit/ Juan Agustin Chaves, Pablo Antonio Abeyta, residents of this pueblo. (pg 76)

22 Nov 1845 – **Juan Antonio Lucero**, legit s/ Manuel Antonio Lucero, deceased, and Maria Casilda Mestas, residents of Ojo Caliente, m. **Maria Feliciana Galbis**, resident of same place, legit d/ Juan Galbis, deceased, and Maria Ygnes Martines; pad/ Antonio Domingo Lucero and Maria Antonia Valdes; wit/ Esteban Chaves and Pablo Antonio Abeyta. (pg 76b)

23 Nov 1845 – **Jose Manuel Varela**, resident of Abiquiu, widower of Maria Teodora Garduño, deceased, m. **Maria Manuela Garcia**, resident of same place, legit d/ Antonio Jose Garcia, deceased, and Gertrudis Martines; pad/ Jesus Vigil and Maria Barbara Gallegos; wit/ Juan Agustin Chavis and Esteban Chaves. (pg 76b)

17 Dec 1845 – **Juan Antonio Trugillo**, resident of Abiquiu, widower of Maria Josefa Trugillo, deceased, m. **Maria Guadalupe Gonsales**, resident of same place, legit d/ Francisco Gonsales and Maria Andrea de los Chaves, of this jurisdiction; pad/ Jose Antonio Chaves and Maria de Jesus Martines; wit/ Antonio Abeyta and Juan Agustin Chaves. (pg 76b)

17 Dec 1845 – **Juan de los Reyes Trugillo**, legit s/ Profero Trugillo and Maria Juana Trugillo, residents of this pueblo, m. **Maria Encanasion Trugillo**, resident of same pueblo, natural d/ Maria Manuela Trugillo; pad/ Martin Martines and Maria Manuela Valdes, of Abiquiu; wit/ Juan Agustin Chaves and Esteban Chaves. (pg 77)

17 Dec 1845 – **Miguel Antonio Madrid**, resident of this parish, widower of Maria Josefa Duran, deceased, m. **Maria Casilda Suares**, resident of Abiquiu, legit d/ Pedro Suares and Maria de la Luz Garcia; pad/ Antonio Mansanares and Maria Antonia Madrid; wit/ Juan Agustin Chaves and Francisco Estban Chaves. (pg 77)

17 Oct 1845 – **Pedro Antonio Madrid**, resident of Abiquiu, legit s/ Julian Madrid and Maria Margarita Quintana, residents of this parish, m. **Maria Luisa Garcia**, resident of same place, legit d/ Lorenso Garcia and Maria Dolores Lucero; pad/ Miguel Madrid and Maria Canuta Suares; wit/ Juan Agustin Chaves and Pablo Antonio Abieta. (pg 77/77b)

4 Jan 1846 – **Pedro Rafael Trugillo**, resident of Abiquiu, legit s/ Pedro Trugillo and Maria Antonia Sanches, deceased, residents of Abiquiu, m. **Maria Nestora Chacon**, resident of this Pueblo, widow of Francisco Antonio Jaramillo; pad/ Juan Ysidro Valdes and Maria Manuela Valdes, residents of this pueblo; wit/ Francisco Esteban Chaves and Pablo Antonio Abeita. (pg 77b)

4 Jan 1846 – **Antonio Jesus Salasar**, legit s/ Jose Salasar, deceased, and Paula Samora, residents of this parish, m. **Maria Dolores Salasar**, resident of same place, legit d/ Tomas Salasar and Maria Manuela Romero; pad/ Lusiano Archuleta and Barbara Lopes, residents of this pueblo; wit/ Francisco Esteban Chaves and Pablo Antonio Abeita. (pg 77b/78)

8 Feb 1846 – **Valtasar Martin**, legit s/ Manuel Martin and Mariana Sanches, residents of this parish, m. **Maria Ygnes Archuleta**, resident of same place, legit d/ Nestor Archuleta and Candelaria Martines; pad/ Ygnacio Archuleta and Maria Guadalupe Sanches, residents of this pueblo; wit/ Juan Agustin Chaves and Francisco Estban Chaves. (pg 78)

7 Mar 1846 – **Jose Miguel Martines**, legit s/ Jose Martines and Maria Dolores Archuleta, residents of this church, m. **Maria Agapita Martines**, resident of same place, legit d/ Jose Martines and Soledad Sanches; pad/ Jose Miguel Ruibal and Maria Antonia Martin; wit/ Pablo Antonio Abeita and Juan Agustin Chaves. (pg 78/78b)

8 Mar 1846 – **Antonio Jose Ramaldo Martines**, legit s/ Jose Martines and Maria Petrona Valdez, deceased, residents of the plaza Blanca, m. **Maria Francisca Salasar**, resident of same place, legit d/ Jose Manuel Salasar, deceased, and Maria Bibiana Sisneros; pad/ Jose Maria Chaves and Maria de Jesus Martines, residents of this pueblo; wit/ Francisco Esteban Chaves and Juan Agustin Chaves. (pg 78b)

26 Mar 1846 – **Juan Salbador Madrid**, legit s/ Juan Madrid, deceased, and Maria de Jesus Martinez, residents of el Rito, m. **Maria Manuela Manasares**, resident of same place, legit d/ Jose Antonio Manasares and Maria Dolores Abila; pad/ Juan Jose Martines and Maria Josefa Martines, of el Rito; wit/ Pablo Antonio Abieta and Francisco Esteban Chavez. (pg 78b/79)

26 Mar 1846 – **Nemecio de Jesus Lucero**, legit s/ Juan de Jesus Lucero, deceased, and Maria Getrudis Archuleta, residents of el Rito, m. **Maria Manuela Valdes**, resident of same place, widow of Santiago Santisteban; pad/ Bitero Archuleta and Maria Francisa Salasar of el Rito; wit/ Francisco Esteban Chaves and Pablo Abeita of Rito. (pg 79)

11 Jun 1846 – **Rafael Valdez**, resident of Ojo Caliente, widower of Ana Maria Chaves, m. **Maria Pelegrina Martines**, resident of same place, widow of Jose Rafael Sisneros; pad/ Pedro

Luis Lujan and Anna Maria Jaramillo; wit/ Francisco Esteban Chavez and Juan Agustin Chaves. (pg 79/79b)

23 Aug 1846 – **Jose Manuel Martines**, widower of 1st marriage to Maria Juana Valdes, m. **Maria Luysa Mestas,** all residents of Ojo Caliente, widow of Jose Manuel Atensio; pad/ Felipe Lopes and Maria Ysabel Mestas, residents of this pueblo; wit/ Juan Agustin Chaves and Pablo Antonio Abeyta. (pg 79b)

27 Sep 1846 – **Nicolas Archuleta**, legit s/ Jose Miguel Archuleta and Maria Isabel Casado, residents of the plaza of San Juan Nepomuceno of el Rito, m. **Maria Manuela Manchego**, resident of same place, legit d/ Manuel Estevan Manchego and Maria Ramona Espinosa; pad/ Melquiades Antonio Montaño and Maria Manuela Montaño, residents of this pueblo; wit/ Juan Agustin Chaves and Pablo Antonio Abeyta. (pg 80)

14 Oct 1846 – **Juan Jose Gallegos**, legit s/ Rafael Antonio Gallegos and Maria Josefa Martines, residents Ojo Caliente, m. **Maria Paula Gomes**, resident of el Rito, legit d/ Jose Pedro Gomes and Maria Manuela Martines; pad/ Jose Felis Galvis and Maria Manuela Chacon, residents of Ojo Caliente; wit/ Juan Agustin Chaves and Pablo Antonio Abeuta. (pg 80/80b)

~~1 Nov 1846 – Jose Ysbel Lopez m. Maria Dolores Chabes, originally of Rito~~ (pg 80b) Entry made in the book and then crossed out

1 Nov 1846 – **Jose Ysabel Lopes**, legit s/ Ramon Lopes and Maria Lugarda Espinosa, native and residents of el Rito, m. **Maria Gregoria Chavez**, resident of same place, legit d/ Antonio Chavez, deceased, and Maria Estefana Lucero; pad/ El Señor Diacon, Vicente S. Montaño and Maria Rosa Montaño, residents of Rito; wit/ Pablo Lucero and Jose Antonia Martines. (pg 81)

1 Nov 1846 – **Jose Rumaldo Mansanares**, legit s/ Jose Antonio Mansanares and Maria de la Luz Madrid, natives and residents of Abiqiui, m. **Maria Juanita Martines**, resident of same place, legit d/ Jose Alvino Martines and Maria de Marta Garcia; pad/ Jose Manuel Chaves and Maria Feliciana Gallegos, residents of the same place; wit/ Rafael Trugillo and Jose Pablo Trujillo. (pg 81/81b)

2 Dec 1846 – **Juan de Jesus Salasar**, legit s/ Jose Miguel Salasar, deceased, and Maria Manuela Derrera, residents of Abiqiui, m. **Juana Maria Crispin**, resident of el Rito, legit d/ Jose Miguel Crispin, deceased, and Maria Relles Chaves; pad/ Jose Maria Baca and Maria Ygnacia Chaves, residents of el Rito; wit/ , Juan Agustin Marin and Mariano Baldes. (pg 81b/82)

4 Dec 1846 – **Juan Andres Mansanares**, legit s/ Manuel Mansanares and Maria Sencion Sandobal, originally of Abiquiu and of El Rito, m. **Juana Maria Sisneros**, resident of la Puente,

legit d/ Roman Sisneros and Maria del Carmen Ortega; pad/ Antonio Domingo Martines and Maria Alta Gracia Garcia, residents of la Puente. (pg 82)

4 Dec 1846 – **Juan de Jesus Romero**, single legit s/ Francisco Romero and Maria Dolores Lopez, deceased, m. **Maria Ysabel Martinez**, single, legit d/ Juan Cristobal Martines and Maria Josefa Alarid; pad/ Antonio Martines and Maria Andres Garcia, residents of la Puente; wit/ Juan Agustin Chaves and Pablo Abeyta. (pg 82/82b)

4 Dec 1846 – **Antonio Maria Salas**, legit s/ Jose Rafael Salas, deceased, and Maria Miguela de la Crus Martin, m. **Maria Antonia Lobato**, resident of Ojo Caliente, legit d/ Migel Antonio Lobato and Maria Francisca Mansanares. (pg 82b)

23 Jan 1847 – **Agapito Martines**, legit s/ Ygnacio Martines and Maria Josefa Trugillo, orignally of Abiquiu and residents of el Rito of Chama, m. **Maria Rufina Salasar**, resident of this parish, legit d/ Salbador Salasar and Maria Ypolita Gallegos; pad/ Migel Antonio Galles and Maria Madalena Gallegos, residents of San Rafael of Rialito; wit/ Mariano Baldcs and Santiago Trugillo. (pg 82b/83)

23 Jan 1847 – **Francisco Antonio Espinosa**, legit s/ Antonio Espinosa and Maria Jetrudes Archuleta, residents of el Rito, m. **Anamaria Baldes,** single legit d/ Antonio Jose Baldes, deceased, and Maria Soledad Martin; pad/ Juan Antonio Espinosa and Maria Manuela Gomes, residents of Taos; wit/ Mariano Valdes and Jose Pablo Antonio Abeyta. (pg 83)

7 Mar 1847 – **Jose Benito Salasar,** originally of the mission of Santa Clara, widower of 1st marriage to Agapita Archuleta, deceased, m. **Maria Dolores Lopes,** originally of San Juan de los Caballeros and now of Abiquiu, widow of 1st marriage to Jose Francisco Vigil; pad/ Antonio Ortis and Maria Soledad Salasar, all from Santa Clara; wit/ Jose Polito Serrano and Jose Mariano Serrano. (pg 83/83b)

14 Mar 1847 – **Francisco Estevan Ruibal**, legit s/ Tomas de Jesus Ruibal and Maria Josefa Espinosa, m. **Maria Guadalupe Chacon**, resident of this parish, legit d/ Juan de Jesus Chacon, deceased, and Maria Sencion Martin; pad/ Jose Patricio Chaves and Maria Encarnacion Chaves, of the same place; wit/ Pablo Antonio Abeyta and Santiago Martin. (pg 83b)

14 Mar 1847 – **Jose Manuel Sanches**, legit s/ Jose Antonio Sanches, deceased, and Viviana de Luna, m. **Maria Ysabel Martin,** all residents of this parish, legit d/ Jose Manuel Martin, deceased, and Dolores Jaramillo; pad/ Jose Martines and Anamaria Abeyta, all residents of the same parish; wit/ Pablo Antonio Abeyta and Santiago Martin. (pg 84)

27 Mar 1847 – **Juan Salasar**, legit s/ Jose Manuel Salasar, deceased, and Maria Biviana Sisneros, m. **Maria Margarita Martines**, resident of this church, widow of 1st marriage to Antonio Lopes, deceased; pad/ Antonio Martines and Maria Andrea Garcia, of the same place; wit/ Jose Rafael Martines and Jose Pablo Salasar. (pg 84)

27 Apr 1847 – **Juan Antonio Romero**, legit s/ Tomas Romero, deceased, and Maria Paula deceased, m. **Maria de la Lus Gonsales,** all residents of this church, legit d/ Pascual Gonsales, deceased, and Maria Valentina Trugillo; pad/ Migel Salasar and Maria Benigna Salasar, of this church. (pg 84b)

27 Apr 1847 – **Jose Pascual Maese** of Ojo Caliente, widower of Maria Josefa Lucero, deceased, m. **Maria Ysabel Trugillo**, resident of Ojo Caliente, legit d/ Jose Trugillo, deceased, and Maria Antonia Jaramillo; pad/ Eusabio Trugillo and Maria Paula Maese, of the same place; wit/ Mariano Valdes and Santiago Martin. (pg 84b/85)

27 Apr 1847 – **Julian Gallegos**, resident of this parish, widower of Maria Salome Salasar, m. **Maria Antonia Martin**, natural d/ Maria Guadalupe Martin, deceased; pad/ Ramon Cordova and Maria Antonia Quintana, of the plaza of la Puente; wit/ Jose Pablo Abeita and Rafael Trugillo. (pg 85)

13 Sep 1847 – **Juan Pablo Valdes**, resident of this parish, legit s/ Jose Valdes and Maria Antonia Baros, m. **Maria Encarnacion de Luna**, resident of the plaza de Blanca, legit d/ Juan de Jesus de Luna and Maria Francisca Garcia; pad/ Jose Andres Trugillo and Maria Altagracia Martinez, residents of this pueblo; wit/ Pablo Abeyta and Santiago Trugillo. (pg 85/85b)

28 Sep 1847 – **Antonio Maria Jaramillo**, legit s/ Patricio Jaramillo, deceased, and Maria Francisca Olguin, deceased, residents of el Rito, m. **Maria Guadalupe Gallegos**, resident of the same place, legit d/ Manuel Gallegos and Maria de la Luz Martines; pad/ Francisco Vigil and Maria Serafina Vigil, of the same place; wit/ Pablo Abeyta and Eulogino Alarid. (pg 85b)

28 Sep 1847 – **Jose Manuel Gutierres**, legit s/ Antonio Gutierres, deceased, and Maria Francisca Martin, residents of this Pueblo, m. **Maria Rumalda Naranjo**, resident of el Rito, legit d/ Noberto Naranjo and Maria de Jesus Valdez; pad/ Diego Naranjo and Maria Gregoria Naranjo, of the same place; wit/ Pablo Abeyta and Juan Jose Alarid. (pg 86)

8 Jan 1848 – **Pedro Antonio Sisneros**, legit s/ Alejandro Sisneros and Angela Vigil, residents of el Rito, m. **Maria Trinidad Martines**, resident of the same place, legit d/ Julian Martines and Catarida Ortis, deceased; pad/ Eusebio Martines and Maria Josefa Chaves, residents of the same place; wit/ Pablo Antonio Abeyta and Santiago Trugillo. (pg 86/86b)

8 Jan 1848 – **Jesus Maria Olguin**, resident of Ojo Caliente, legit s/ Antonio Jose Olguin, deceased, and Maria Magdalena Mascareñas, residents of Ojo Caliente, m. **Maria Soledad Valdes**, resident of Ojo Caliente, legit d/ Rafael Valdes and Juana Maria Chaves, deceased; pad/ Mariano Valdes and Maria Manuela Maese; wit/ Pablo Antonio Abeyta and Rafael Trugillo. (pg 86b)

8 Jan 1848 – **Juan Balentin Archuleta**, resident of Ojo Caliente, legit s/ Antonio Casimiro Archuleta and Maria Monserrate de Leal, residents of this church, m. **Maria Ysabel Teodora Martin**, resident of Ojo Caliente, legit d/ Pablo Martin, deceased, and Maria Concepcion Romero; pad/ Eusebio Valdes and Maria Dolores Chacon; wit/ Juan Jose Alarid and Pablo Antonio Abeyta. (pg 86b/87)

8 Jan 1848 – **Jose Tomas Romero**, legit s/ Francisco Romero and Maria Dolores Lopes, deceased, m. **Margarita Solome Martin**, all residents of this parish, natural d/ Maria Josefa Martin; pad/ Francisco Lopes and Concepsion Suaso, of Abiquiu; wit/ Juan Jose Alarid and Pablo Antonio Abcyta. (pg 87)

8 Jan 1848 – **Jose Rafael Garcia**, legit s/ Antonio Jose Garcia, deceased, and Maria Antonia Martin, m. **Micaela Madrid**, legit d/ Cristobal Madrid and Josefa del Castillo; pad/ Pedro Lopes and Maria Francisca Valdes; wit/ Pablo Antonio Abeyta and Jose Santiago Trugillo. (pg 87b)

8 Feb 1848 – **Antonio Serafin Peña**, resident of Ojo Caliente, legit s/ Pedro Peña, deceased, and Maria del Carmel Jiron, m. **Maria Liodocia Ruibal**, resident of Ojo Caliente, legit d/ Jose Ruibal and Antonia Maria Gallegos, deceased; pad/ Mariano Peña and Maria Guadalupe Trugillo; wit/ Rafael Trugillo and Pablo Antonio Abeyta. (pg 87b/88)

8 Feb 1848 – **Jose Manuel Martinez**, resident of el Rito, legit s/ Julian Martinez and Maria Catarina Ortiz, deceased, m. **Maria Nicolasa Valdes**, resident of Ojo Caliente, legit d/ German Valdes, deceased, and Maria Josefa Gomes; pad/ Juan Maria Vigil and Maria Salome Vigil; wit/ Felipe Gallegos and Pablo Antonio Abeyta. (pg 88)

20 Feb 1848 – **Jose Nasario Valdes**, resident of Ojo Caliente, legit s/ Mariano Valdes, deceased, and Maria Manuela Mes, m. **Maria Paula Duran**, resident of Ojo Caliente, legit d/ Jose Duran and Maria de la Luz Fernandes; pad/ Juan Ysidro Suaso and Maria Guadalupe Sisneros; wit/ Pablo Antonio Abeyta and Santiago Trugillo. (pg 88/88b)

22 Feb 1848 – **Francisco Tomas Baca**, resident of Abiquiu, widower of Maria Manuela Ortis, m. **Maria Ruperta Gallegos**, residents of Ojo Caliente, widow of 1st marriage to Ricardo Lucero, deceased; pad/ Nicolas Lusero and Maria Manuela Archuleta; wit/ Francisco Salasar and Pablo Antonio Abeyta. (pg 88b/89)

22 Feb 1848 – **Jose Vicente de Herrera**, legit s/ Cristobal de Herrera and Maria Soledad Vigil, residents of Chama, m. **Maria Rufina Abeyta**, resident of Barranca, legit d/ Miguel Antonio Abeyta and Maria Rosa Vigil; pad/ Antonio Vigil and Maria Soledad Salasar; wit/ Juan Jose Alarid and Geronimo Gallegos. (pg 89)

8 Mar 1848 – **Antonio Casias**, resident of el Rito, legit s/ Jose Encarnacion Casias and Maria del Carmel Martines, m. **Maria Tiodora Velarde**, resident of el Rito, legit d/ Juan Luis Velarde and Guadalupe Martines; pad/ Felipe Casias and Vibiana Lusero; wit/ Manuel Ortega and Pablo Antonio Abeyta. (pg 89/89b)

8 Mar 1848 – **Bibian Montoya**, natural s/ Maria Rosalia Montoya, m. **Ana Maria Valdes**, resident of Abiquiu, legit d/ Antonio Jose Valdes and Maria Soledad Martines, residents of Abiquiu; pad/ Antonio Manzanarez Mares and Maria Manuela Valdes; wit/ Jose Luna and Manuel Valdes. (pg 89b)

3 Mar 1848 – **Juan Jose Alarid**, legit s/ Gregorio Alarid and Maria Paula Romero, m. **Maria de Refugio Duran**, resident of Abiquiu, widow of Antonio Jose Salasar; pad/ Juan Nepomuceno Valdes and Maria Vicenta Archuleta; wit/ Pablo Antonio Abeyta and Antonio Ortiz. (pg 90)

3 Mar 1848 – **Francisco Moreno**, resident of Ojo Caliente, legit s/ Antonio Moreno, deceased, and Maria Joaquina Olguin, m. **Maria Aguilar**, resident of Ojo Caliente, legit d/ Pablo Aguilar, deceased, and Maria Juliana Naranjo; wit/ Pablo Antonio Abeyta and Felipe Gallegos. (pg 90/90b)

21 Dec 1847 – **Mariano Barela**, resident of el Rito, legit s/ Diego Antonio Barela, deceased, and Maria de la Lus Naranjo, of Abiquiu, m. **Maria Bibiana Moya**, resident of el Rito, natural d/ Maria Concepcion Moya; pad/ Francisco Vigil and Maria Alcadia Salasar; wit/ Rafael Trugillo and Pablo Antonio Abeyta. (pg 90b)

10 Mar 1848 – **Simon Martines**, resident of el Rito, legit s/ Jose Francisco Martines, deceased, and Maria Pascuala Jiron, resident of el Rito, m. **Maria Decideria Martin**, resident of same place, legit d/ Antonio Martin and Maria Josefa Sanches; pad/ Felipe Martines and Maria Antonia Garcia; wit/ Geronimo Gallegos and Pablo Antonio Abeyta. (pg 90b/91)

10 Mar 1848 – **Juan de los Reyes Garcia**, resident of the Pueblo, legit s/ Antonio Garcia, deceased, and Maria Teresa Trugillo, m. **Maria Guadalupe Trugillo**, resident of this Pueblo, legit d/ Ygnacio Trugillo, deceased, and Maria Rita Valdes; pad/ Juan de Dios Olibari and Maria Gregorio Lujan; wit/ Esteban Chaves and Manuela Ortega. (pg 91)

12 Apr 1848 – **Juan Nepomuceno Trugillo**, resident of this Pueblo, legit s/ Jose Manuel Trugillo, deceased, and Maria Maurina Martin, m. **Maria Salome Jaramillo**, resident of this Pueblo, widow of Juan Agustin Jaramillo; pad/ Juan Cristobal Lugan and Maria Josefa Jageva; wit/ Jose Santiago Trugillo and Pablo Antonio Abeyta. (pg 91b)

12 Apr 1848 – **Jose Secilio Montolla**, resident of Ojo Caliente, natural s/ Maria de la Lus Montolla, deceased, m. **Maria Juliana Romero**, legit d/ Tomas Romero, deceased, and Maria del Rosario Romero; pad/ Antonio J. Salasar; wit/ Pablo Antonio Abeyta and Jose Santiago Trugillo. (pg 91b)

19 Apr 1848 – **Jose Tomas Garcia**, resident of the Pueblo, a/ Miguel Garcia and Rumalda de Herrera, m. **Maria Candelaria Quintana**, resident of this Pueblo, legit d/ Jose Antonio Quintana, deceased, and Ana Maria Lujan; pad/ Juan Domingo Quintana and Maria Dolores Garcia; wit/ Manuel Ortega and Pablo Antonio Abeyta. (pg 92)

26 Apr 1848 – **Benigno Mes**, resident of Ojo Caliente, legit s/ Juan Manuel Macs, deceased, and Maria Polonia Aragon, m. **Martia Rugina Rodrigues**, resident of Ojo Caliente, legit d/ Jose Rafael Rodrigues, deceased, and Faustina Lucero; pad/ Juan Ysidro Lucero and Maria Bentura Gallegos; wit/ Manuel Ortega and Pablo Antonio Abeyta. (pg 92/92b)

22 Apr 1848 – **Jose Miguel Gallegos**, resident of Ojo Caliente, widower of Margarita Lucero, deceased, m. **Maria Antonia Trugillo**, resident of Ojo Caliente, widow of Francisco Martin, deceased; pad/ Antonio Ysabel Gallegos and Maria Ygnacia Martin, residents of the same place; wit/ Manuel Ortega and Pablo Antonio Abeyta. (pg 92b)

22 Apr 1848 – **Pedro Ygnacio Martines**, resident of the Pueblo, legit s/ Francisco Martines and Maria Bernardina Martines, residents of the Pueblo, m. **Maria de los Angeles Padilla**, resident of the same place, legit d/ Santo Padilla and Maria Josefa Trugillo; pad/ Felipe Gallegos and Maria Marselina Gallegos; wit/ Geronimo Gallegos and Jose Santiago Trugillo. (pg 92b/93)

27 May 1848 – **Juan Nepomuseno Valdes**, resident of Ojo Caliente, widower of 1st marriage to Maria Vicenta Archuleta, deceased, m. **Juana Maria Archuleta**, resident of the same place, legit d/ Jose Archuleta and Maria Juana Mansanares; pad/ Jose Ygnacio Salasar and Maria Juliana Montoya; wit/ Pablo Antonio Abeyta and Rafael Trujillo. (pg 93)

18 Jun 1848 – **Jose Francisco Sandobal**, resident of Ojo Caliente, widow of Anna Maria Ortega, m. **Maria Francisca Archuleta**, resident of Ojo Caliente, legit d/ Miguel Archuleta, deceased, and Maria de la Lus Martines; pad/ Seberino Martines; wit/ Pablo Antonio Abeyta and Jose Manuel Valdes. (pg 93b)

8 Aug 1848 – **Jose Julian Trugillo**, resident of the Pueblo, legit s/ Rafael Trugillo, deceased, and Maria Martina Griego, m. **Ana Maria Valdes**, resident of the capilla, legit d/ Eusebio Valdes and Maria Manuela Martines; pad/ Guadalupe Gallegos and Maria Barbara Trugillo; wit/ Pablo Antonio Abeyta and Felipe Gallegos. (pg 93b/94)

8 Aug 1848 – **Jose Vicente Abila**, resident of el Rito, natural s/ Maria Josefa Abila, resident of el Rito, m. **Maria Nestora Lucero**, resident of the same place, legit d/ Juan Agustin Lucero, deceased, and Maria de la Lus Sanchez; pad/ Miguel Trugillo and Maria del Carmel Casillas, of el Rito; wit/ Pablo Antonio Abeyta and Esteban Chaves. (pg 94/94b)

16 Sep 1848 – **Juan Nepomuseno Castelo**, resident of Barrano, legit s/ Mariano Castelo and Ysidora Ortega, m. **Maria Nieves Trugillo**, resident of this Pueblo, natural d/ Concepcion Trugillo; pad/ Juan Nepomuseno Valdes and Juana Maria Archuleta; wit/ Pablo Abeyta and Juan Esteban Chaves. (pg 94b)

16 Sep 1848 – **Antonio Jose Belasques**, resident of el Rito, widower of 1st marriage to Maria Antonia Martines, m. **Juana Maria Lopes**, resident of el Rito, legit d/ Baltasar Lopes, deceased, and Consepcion Abila; pad/ Diego Madrid and Rosalia Gallegos, residents of the same place; wit/ Pablo Antonio Abeyta and Rafael Trujillo. (pg 94b/95)

16 Sep 1848 – **Jose Gabriel Belasques**, resident of Questa, legit s/ Juaquin Belasques and Maria Antonia Rosa Romero, m. **Maria Leonora Martines**, resident of Rito, legit d/ Jose Maria Martines, deceased, and Maria Micaela Valdes, all residents of this parish; pad/ Jose Maria Atencio and Anna Maria Baldes; wit/ Francisco Esteban Chaves and Santiago Trugillo. (pg 95)

24 Sep 1848 – **Juan Jose Deaguero**, resident of Santa Clara, widower of Maria Asencion Salasar, m. **Maria Guadalupe Gomes**, resident of el Rito, legit d/ Fileto Gomes and Maria Encarnacion Sanches; pad/ Pedro Gomes and Maria Antonia Martin, residents of el Rito; wit/ Francisco Esteban Chaves and Felipe Gallegos. (pg 95/95b)

19 Nov 1848 – **Vicente Archuleta**, resident of el Rito, legit s/ Antonio Abad Archuleta and Maria Antonia Ribera, m. **Maria Aniceta de Herrera**, resident of el Rito, legit d/ Pedro Antonio de Herrera and Maria Ursula Trugillo; pad/ Geronimo Jaramillo and Maria Aniceta Gallegos; wit/ Francisco Esteban Chaves and Francisco Salasar. (pg 95b/96)

12 Nov 1848 – **Antonio de Jesus Valdes**, resident of Ojo Caliente, legit s/ Jose Manuel Valdes and Maria de la Lus Trugillo, m. **Maria de Jesus Lucero**, resident of Ojo Caliente, legit d/ Vicente Lucero, deceased, and Maria Juliana Maes; pad/ Jose Manuel Vigil and his wife; wit/ Pablo Antonio Abeyta and Manuel Ortega. (pg 96/96b)

10 Nov 1848 – **Jose Maria Torres**, resident of la Sienega, legit s/ Bernardo Torres and Maria Gertrudis Jaques, deceased, m. **Maria Ygnacia Valdes**, resident of el Rito, legit d/ Francisco Valdes and Maria Jasinta Trugillo; pad/ Martin Trugillo and Juana Gallegos; wit/ Pablo Abeyta and Rafael Gallegos. (pg 96b)

22 Nov 1848 – **Juan Andres Gomes**, resident of el Rito, legit s/ Pedro Gomes and Maria Manuela Martin, residents of el Rito, m. **Maria de Jesus Martines**, resident of this parish, legit d/ Cristobal Martines, deceased, and Alaria Josefa Alarid; pad/ Pedro Espinosa and his wife; wit/ Pablo Antonio Abeyta and Francisco Esteban Chaves. (pg 97)

22 Nov 1848 – **Jose Luisano Trugillo**, legit s/ Rafael Trugillo and Trinidad Valdes, residents of this Pueblo, m. **Maria Faustina Sandobal**, widow of 1st marriage to Albino Torres, deceased; pad/ Guadalupe Gallegos and Maria Barbara (left blank); wit/ Jose Santiago Trugillo and Rafael Gallegos. (pg 97/97b)

22 Nov 1848 – **Jose Maria de Noriega**, legit s/ Jose Miguel de Noriega and Juana Maria Ramires, m. **Maria Pabla Espinosa**, legit d/ Ramon Espinosa and Antonia Ygnacia Archuleta; wit/ Francisco Esteban Chaves and Jose Pedro Chaves. (pg 97b)

22 Nov 1848 – **Jose Maria Torres**, legit s/ Carlos Torres and Josefa Valdes, m. **Maria Antonia Archuleta**, single legit d/ Miguel Archuleta, deceased, and Maria de la Luz Martin; pad/ Jose Antonio Belasques and Estefana Martines, residents of Ojo Caliente; wit/ Juan Agustin Chaves and Pablo Abeyta. (pg 97b/98)

22 Nov 1848 – **Jose Agapito Atencio**, resident of Ojo Caliente, legit s/ Francisco Antonio Atencio and Maria Dolores Martines, m. **Maria Josefa Trugillo**, resident of Ojo Caliente, legit d/ Jose Maria Trugillo and Marselina Ruibali; pad/ Miguel Martin and Maria Francisca Ruibali; wit/ Manuel Ortega and Francisco Esteban Chaves. (pg 98)

26 Nov 1848 – **Juan Santos Samora**, resident of la Puente, natural s/ Encarnacion Samora, m. **Maria Manuela Salasar**, resident of the same place, legit d/ Juan Felipe Salasar and Maria Gertrudis Suazo; pad/ Sabino Salasar and Maria Rufina Lopes; wit/ Juan Agustin Chaves and Antonio Ortega. (pg 98b)

2 Dec 1848 – **Jose Manuel Vigil**, resident of el Rito, servant of Ramon Vigil and Maria Catarina Montoya, m. **Maria Guadalupe Samora**, resident of el Rito, legit d/ Juan de Jesus Samora and Maria Rosalia Mestas, deceased; pad/ Juan Antonio Valdes and Maria Regina Valdes, residents of el Rito; wit/ Francisco Esteban Chaves and Juan Agustin Chaves. (pg 98b/99)

2 Dec 1848 – **Jose Andres Trugillo**, legit s/ Pedro Trugillo and Maria Antonia Sanches, m. **Maria Juana Garcia**, legit d/ Jose Pablo Garcia, deceased, and Maria Gertrudis Abeyta; pad/ Francisco Salasar and Maria Soledad Salasar, residents of Chama; wit/ Pablo Antonio Abeyta and Jose Antonio Mansanares. (pg 99)

11 Dec 1848 – **Jose Francisco Aragon**, legit s/ Antonio Vivian Aragon, deceased, and Maria de la Lus Lucero, m. **Maria Clara Chaves**, resident of Servilleta, legit d/ Eusebio Chaves, deceased, and Ysabel Jaques; pad/ Jose Gregorio Ruis and Maria Guadalupe Ruis; wit/ Francisco Esteban Chaves and Jose Pedro Chaves. (pg 99/99b)

11 Dec 1848 – **Jose Tomas Sanches**, resident of la Cueva, legit s/ Ramon Sanches and Maria Lionisia Lobato, m. **Maria Soledad Abeyta**, resident of la Cueva, legit d/ Jose Ygnacio Abeyta and Maria Manuela Trugillo; pad/ Eulogio Gallegos and Albina Chacon; wit/ Francisco Esteban Chaves and Pablo Antonio Abeyta. (pg 99b/100)

11 Dec 1848 – **Antonio Lopes**, resident of el Rito, legit s/ Valtazar Lopes, deceased, and Maria Concepcion Abila, m. **Maria de Trinidad Valdes**, resident of el Rito, legit d/ Antonio Valdes and Maria Concepcion Montoya; pad/ Juan de Jesus Trugillo and Maria Bitalia Trugillo, residents of el Rito; wit/ Pablo Antonio Abeyta and Manuel Ortega. (pg 100)

17 Dec 1848 – **Jose Manuel Baca**, single legit s/ Rafael Baca, deceased, and Maria Biviana Martines, m. **Maria Antonia Madrid**, legit d/ Miguel Antonio Madrid and Maria Josefa Abeyta, deceased, residents of Tierra Azul; pad/ Pedro Trugillo and Maria Altagracia Martines, residents of same place; wit/ Francisco Esteban Chaves and Pablo Antonio Abeyta. (pg 100/100b)

18 Mar 1849 – **Candelario Lujan**, resident of this Pueblo, legit s/ Necolas Lujan and Soledad Romero, m. **Maria Encarnacion Martines**, resident of this Pueblo, widow of 1st marriage to Miguel Alarid; pad/ Manuel Salasar and Maria Delubina Salasar; wit/ Juan Agustin Chaves and Esteban Chaves. (pg 100b/101)

18 Aug 1849 – **Eulogio Seguaro**, resident of Cañones, widower of 1st marriage to Maria Sabina Baca, m. **Maria Bitazia Valdes**, legit d/ Jose Miguel Valdes, deceased, and Maria Francisca Mestas; pad/ Ygnacio Archuleta and Guadalupe Sanches; wit/ Francisco Esteban Chaves and Manuel Ortega. (pg 101)

22 Jun 1849 – **Rafael Gallegos**, resident of el Rito, legit s/ Domingo Gallegos, deceased, and Maria Concepcion Balasques, m. **Maria del Refugio Romero**, resident of el Rito, legit d/ Pablo Romero, deceased, and Maria Pabla Gomes; pad/ Fernando Martin and Maria Montaño, residents of el Rito; wit/ Jose Maria Montaño and Diego Madrid. (pg 101/101b)

28 Jun 1849 – **Jose de los Relles Gallegos**, resident of Ojo Caliente, widower of 1st marriage to Serafina Vigil, m. **Maria Crisanta Trugillo**, resident of el Rito, legit d/ Jose Trugillo, deceased, and Maria Esquipula Valdes; pad/ Miguel Martin and Maria Francisca Ruibali, residents of the same place; wit/ Francisco Esteban Chaves and Jose Pedro Chaves. (pg 101b)

28 Jun 1849 – **Jesus Maria Suaso**, resident of Ojo Caliente, legit s/ Antonio Suaso and Maria Dolores Duran, m. **Maria Paubla Archuleta**, all residents of Ojo Caliente, widow of 1st marriage to Gregorio Montoya. (pg 102)

1 Jul 1849 – **Juan Ortis**, legit s/ Salbador Ortis, deceased, and Maria Soledad Baca, m. **Maria Soledad Aguilar**, resident of Ojo Caliente, legit d/ Jose Antonio Aguilar and Maria de la Lus Quintana; pad/ Francisco Lopes and Maria Concepcion Suaso, residents of Barranca; wit/ Juan Esteban Chaves and Juan de Dios Valdes. (pg 102b)

20 Sep 1849 – **Jose Alejandro Madrid**, single legit s/ Antonio Madrid and Francisca Martin, residents of this parish, m. **Maria Rosa Atencio**, resident of same place, widow of Vicente Trujeques; pad/ Francisco Lopes and Concepcion Suaso; wit/ Francisco Esteban Chaves and Juan Agustin Chaves. (pg 102b/103)

22 Sep 1849 – **Juan Andres Trugillo**, resident of Ojo Caliente, legit s/ Jose Maria Trugillo and Maria Marselina Ruibali, deceased, residents of Ojo Caliente, m. **Maria Estefana Valdes**, widow of 1st marriage to Jose Gabriel Valdes; pad/ Juan Cristobal Lujan and Josefa Fageda; wit/ Francisco Esteban Chaves and Juan Agustin Chaves. (pg 103)

1 Oct 1849 – **Pedro Jose Martin**, resident of this Pueblo, legit s/ Ysidro Martin, deceased, and Maria Tomasa Romero, residents of the Pueblo, m. **Maria Ygnacia Padilla**, resident of the same place, legit d/ Alejandro Padilla, deceased, and Maria Manuela Lujan; pad/ Andres Salasar and Maria Soledad Salasar; wit/ Francisco Esteban Chaves and Rafael Gallegos. (pg 103b)

27 Nov 1849 – **Lorenzo Antonio Trugillo**, resident of el Rito, legit s/ Juan de Dios Trugillo and Maria Juana Antonia Martin, residents of el Rito, m. **Maria Ygnacia Montoya**, resident of the same place, legit d/ Fernando de Montoya and Maria Manuela Sisneros; pad/ Geronimo Jaramillo and Yniceta Gallegos, residents of the same place; wit/ Juan Agustin Chaves and Francisco Esteban Chaves. (pg 103b/104)

27 Nov 1849 – **Jose Leonides Galvis**, resident of Ojo Caliente, legit s/ Juan Jose Galvis, deceased, and Maria Ynes Martines, residents of Ojo Caliente, m. **Maria de los Reyes Lobato**, resident of the same place, legit d/ Pedro Antonio Lobato and Maria Concepcion Herrera; pad/ Buenabentura Martin, resident of el Rito; wit/ Francisco Esteban Chaves and Juan Agustin Chaves. (pg 104)

27 Nov 1849 – **Bitoriano Archuleta**, resident of el Rito, legit s/ Jose Miguel de Archuleta and Maria Ysabel Casados, deceased, residents of el Rito, m. **Maria Petrona Gallegos**, resident of el Rito, legit d/ Domingo Gallegos, deceased, and Maria Concepcion Velasquez; pad/ Jose Maria Ballejos and Maria Luisa Archuleta, residents of the same place; wit/ Francisco Esteban Chaves and Juan Agustin Chaves. (pg 104/104b)

27 Nov 1849 – **Jose Maria Valdes**, resident of el Rito, widower of Maria Bibiana Sisneros, resident of el Rito, m. **Maria Pabla Alire**, resident of el Rito, legit d/ Jose Manuel Alire and Maria Dolores Maes; pad/ Felipe Casias and Maria Biviana Lucero; wit/ Francisco Esteban Chaves and Agustin Chaves. (pg 104b)

29 Nov 1849 – **Jose Geronimo Valdes**, resident of Ojo Caliente, legit s/ Jose Ygnacio Valdes and Maria Dolores Olguin, residents of Ojo Caliente, m. **Maria Bibiana de la Ahora**, resident of the same place, legit d/ Santiago de la Ahora and Maria Manuela Marques; pad/ Miguel Martin and Maria Francisa Ruibal; wit/ Francisco Esteban Chaves and Rafael Gallegos. (pg 104b/105)

29 Nov 1849 – **Antonio Maria Archuleta**, resident of Abiquiu, legit s/ Jose Ramon Archuleta and Juana Josefa Lucero, residents of Abiquiu, m. **Maria Serafina Trugillo**, resident of the same place, legit d/ Francisco Antonio Trugillo and Estefana Delgado; pad/ Ramon Cordoba and Maria Antonia Quintana, residents of the same place; wit/ Francisco Esteban Chaves and Felipe Gallegos. (pg 105/105b)

30 Nov 1849 – **Antonio Jose Lucero**, resident of Ojo Caliente, legit s/ Jose Francisco Lucero and Maria de la Lus Chaves, residents of Ojo Caliente, m. **Maria Bernarda Gallegos**, resident of the same place, legit d/ Santiago Gallegos and Maria de la Lus Lucero, deceased; pad/ Jose Francisco Ruibal, resident of Ojo Caliente; wit/ Francisco Esteban Chaves and Juan Agustin Chaves. (pg 105b)

30 Nov 1849 – **Agustin Martines**, resident of Ojo Caliente, legit s/ Esteban Martines and Encarnacion Lucero, residents of Ojo Caliente, m. **Maria Josefa Valdes**, resident of the same place, legit d/ Antonio Valdes and Maria Manuela Lobato, deceased; pad/ Jose Bicente Jaramillo and Maria Salome Ortis, residents of the same place; wit/ Francisco Esteban Chaves and Rafael Gallegos. (pg 105b/106)

30 Nov 1849 – **Ylario Atencio**, resident of Ojo Caliente, legit s/ Pedro Atencio and Maria de Jesus Aguilar, residents of Ojo Caliente, m. **Maria Ysidora Chaves**, resident of Ojo Caliente, legit d/ Juan Antonio Chaves and Maria Encarnacion Lucero; pad/ Miguel Martin and Maria

Francisca Ruibal, residents of the same place; wit/ Francisco Esteban Chaves and Pablo Antonio Abeyta. (pg 106/106b)

30 Nov 1849 – **Bacilio Gallegos**, resident of el Rito, legit s/ Domingo Gallegos, deceased, and Maria Concepcion de Velasques, resident of el Rito, m. **Maria Juana Casias**, resident of el Rito, legit d/ Jose Casias and Maria del Carmel Martinez; pad/ Aquilino Ocano and Estefana Trugillo, residents of the same place; wit/ Francisco Esteban Chaves and Rafael Gallegos. (pg 106b)

30 Nov 1849 – **Francisco Romero**, resident of Barranca, natural s/ Guadalupe Romero, resident of Barranca, m. **Maria Josefa Garcia**, resident of Barranca, natural d/ Guadalupe Garcia; pad/ Luciano Archuleta and Maria Barbara Lopes, residents of Abiquiu; wit/ Francisco Esteban Chaves and Mariano Trugillo. (pg 106b/107)

30 Nov 1849 – **Antonio Maria Garcia**, resident of Ojo Caliente, legit s/ Juan Antonio Garcia and Maria Manuela Trugillo, deceased, resident of Ojo Caliente, m. **Maria Manuela Valdes**, single legit d/ Reyes Valdes, deceased, and Maria de la Lus Vialpando, residents of this parish; pad/ Antonio Gallegos and Maria Antonia Martin, residents of the same place; wit/ Francisco Esteban Chaves and Rafael Gallegos. (pg 107/107b)

30 Nov 1849 – **Jesus Maria Garcia**, resident of Ojo Caliente, legit s/ Salbador Garcia and Candelaria Salasar, resident of Abiquiu, m. **Maria Antonia Trugillo**, resident of same place, legit d/ Esteban Trugillo and Loreta Martin; pad/ Manuel Salasar and Maria Biviana Salasar; wit/ Francisco Esteban Chaves and Juan Agustin Chaves. (pg 107b)

30 Nov 1849 – **Juan Ygnacio Martin**, resident of Cañones, legit s/ Gregorio Martin and Francisca Valdes, residents of los Cañones, m. **Maria de Jesus Serrano**, resident of the same place, legit d/ Manuel Serrano and Maria Dolores Martin; pad/ Jose de la Lus Gallegos and Maria Loreta Gallegos, residents of the same place; wit/ Francisco Esteban Chaves and Felipe Gallegos. (pg 107b/108)

30 Nov 1849 – **Jose Aniceto Espinosa**, resident of el Rito, legit s/ Jose Alejandro Espinosa and Encarnacion Sisneros, deceased, residents of el Rito, m. **Maria Juliana Quintana**, resident of the same place, legit d/ Manuel Quintana and Maria de Rosario Segura; pad/ Geronimo Jaramillo and Eniceta Gallegos; wit/ Francisco Esteban Chaves and Agustin Chaves. (pg 108)

30 Nov 1849 – **Jose Dolores Lucero**, resident of el Rito, legit s/ Juan del Carmel Lucero, deceased, and Maria Rosa Martin, residents of el Rito, m. **Maria Josefa Lopes**, resident of the same place, legit d/ Miguel Lopes and Maria Manuela Mestas; pad/ Juan Bautista Espinosa and Maria Ruperta Lopes, residents of the same place; wit/ Francisco Esteban Chaves and Rafael Gallegos. (pg 108b)

1 Dec 1849 – **Juan Bautista Serrano**, resident of Barranca, legit s/ Hipolito Serrano and Maria Manuela Mestas, residents of Barranca, m. **Maria Beguina Madrid**, resident of the same place, legit d/ Juan Cristobal Madrid and Maria Josefa Moya; pad/ Ygnacio Archuleta and Guadalupe Sanches; wit/ Pablo Antonio Abeyta and Felipe Gallegos. (pg 108b)

1 Dec 1849 – **Antonio de Jesus Duran**, resident of Ojo Caliente, legit s/ Jose Fernando Duran and Maria de la Luz Fernandes, residents of Ojo Caliente, m. **Maria de la Lus Atencio**, resident of the same place, legit d/ Pedro Atencio, deceased, and Maria de Jesus Aguilar; pad/ Juan Gurule and Anna Maria Clara Baca, residents of the same place; wit/ Francisco Esteban Chaves and Rafael Gallegos. (pg 109)

2 <u>Nov</u> 1849 – **Manuel Gregorio Martinez**, resident of la Cueva of Ojo Caliente, legit s/ Baltazar Martinez and Maria Josefa Vialpando, residents of la Cueva of Ojo Caliente, m. **Maria Luzia Abeyta**, resident of the same place, legit d/ Jose Ygnacio Abeyta and Maria Manuela Trugillo; wit/ Francisco Esteban Chaves and Juan Agustin Chaves. (pg 109/109b)

16 Dec 1849 – **Jose Miguel Suaso**, resident of Abiquiu, legit s/ Ygnacio Suaso and Maria Francisca Martines, residents of Barranca, m. **Maria Acencion Abeyta**, resident of la Capia, legit d/ Jose Pablo Abeyta and Maria Rosa Salasar; pad/ Francisco Salasar and Maria Soledad Salasar, residents of Chama; wit/ Francisco Chaves and Rafael Gallegos. (pg 109b)

24 Dec 1849 – **Francisco Antonio Mestas**, resident of Abiquiu, legit s/ Jose Maria Mestas and Maria Dolores Rodrigues, residents of Abiquiu, m. **Maria Guadalupe Abeyta**, resident of same place, natural d/ Maria Francisca Abeyta; pad/ Sabino Salasar and Maria Rufina Lopes, residents of same place; wit/ Francisco Esteban Chaves and Mariano Trugillo. (pg 109b/110)

24 Dec 1849 – **Jose Francisco Manchego**, resident of the Pueblo, legit s/ Jose Francisco Manchego and Maria Manuela Archuleta, residents of the Pueblo, m. **Maria Candelaria Butierres**, resident of the same place, legit d/ Miguel Antonio Butierres and Concepcion Garcia, deceased; pad/ Rafael Gallegos and Maria Salaome Garcia, residents of the same place; wit/ Juan Agustin Chaves and Francisco Esteban Chaves. (pg 110)

5 Jan 1850 – **Juan Abeyta**, resident of el Rito, widower of 1st marriage to Maria Ygnacia Martines, m. **Maria de la Luz Vigil**, resident of el Rito, legit d/ Juan Vigil, deceased, and Anna Maria Trugillo; wit/ Francisco Esteban Chaves and Rafael Gallegos. (pg 110/110b)

5 Jan 1850 – **Jose Deciderio Valdes**, resident of Ojo Caliente, legit s/ Santiago Valdes, deceased, and Maria Gertrudis Gallegos, residents of Ojo Caliente, m. **Maria de Jesus Baca**,

resident of same place, legit d/ Pablo Baca and Maria Guadalupe Lusero; pad/ Rafael Gallegos and Salome Garcia; wit/ Juan Agustin Chaves and Mariano Trugillo. (pg 110b)

5 Jan 1850 – **Manuel Garcia**, resident of Abiquiu, legit s/ Jose Pablo Garcia, deceased, and Maria Gertrudis Abeyta, residents of Barranca, m. **Maria Lidubina Valdes**, resident of Abiquiu, legit d/ Miguel Valdes, deceased, and Maria Guadalupe Romero; pad/ Jose de la Lus Gallegos and Maria Loreta Gallegos, residents of the same place; wit/ Francisco Esteban Chaves and Felipe Gallegos. (pg 111)

20 Jan 1850 – **Jose Polinario Casias**, resident of el Rito, legit s/ Jose de la Encarnacion Casias and Maria del Carmel Martines, residents of el Rito, m. **Maria Guadalupe Martin**, resident of the same place, legit d/ Felipe Martin and Maria Antonia Vigil; wit/ Esteban Chavez and Rafael Gallegos. (pg 111/111b)

26 Jan 1850 – **Antonio Simon Lopez**, resident of la Cacita, legit s/ Juan Cristobal Lopez, deceased, and Maria Manuela Chaves, residents of la Casita, m. **Maria Regina Martines**, resident of the same place, legit d/ Manuel Rafael Martines, deceased, and Mariana Sanches; pad/ Jesus Manuel Martines and Maria de la Lus Lopes, residents of the same place; wit/ Cruz Lujan and Jesus Maria Chaves. (pg 111b)

26 Jan 1850 – **Manuel Gregorio de Herrera**, resident of Abiquiu, widower of 1st marriage to Maria Manuela Vialpando, residents of Abiquiu, m. **Maria Doretea Martines**, resident of the same place, legit d/ Juan Miguel Martines, deceased, and Maria Josefa Olivas; pad/ Manuel Salasar and Maria Delubina Salasar, residents of the Plaza Blanca; wit/ Francisco Esteban Chavez and Felipe Gallegos. (pg 111b/112)

4 Feb 1850 – **Jesus Maria de Herrera**, resident of Abiquiu, legit s/ Juan de la Cruz de Herrera and Maria Juana Romero, deceased, residents of Santa Clara, m. **Maria Francisca Martin**, resident of Abiquiu, widow of 1st marriage to Juan Manuel Cordoba; pad/ Matias Vigil and Maria Salome Vigil, residents of Chama; wit/ Jose Maria Montaño and Fernando Montaño. (pg 112)

6 Feb 1850 – **Donaciano Espinosa**, resident of el Rito, legit s/ Antonio Espinosa and Maria Gertrudiz Archuleta, residents of el Rito, m. **Maria Flora Trugillo**, resident of el Rito, legit d/ Julian Trugillo and Maria Nepomusena Gallegos; pad/ Francisco Espinosa and Maria Manuela Baldez, residents of same place; wit/ Francisco Esteban Chavez and Rafael Gallegos. (pg 112/112b)

6 Feb 1850 – **Antonio Maria Narsiso Vigil**, resident of Abiquiu, legit s/ Francisco Esteban Vigil and Maria Candelaria Mestas, deceased, residents of the church of San Juan, m. **Maria Manuela**

Chavez, resident of the church of Abiquiu, legit d/ Jose Maria Chavez and Maria de Jesus Martin; pad/ Jose Benito Zalazar and Maria Dolores Lopes, residents of the same place; wit/ Francisco Esteban Chavez and Pedro Salasar. (pg 112b)

9 Sep 1850 – **priest notations as to Archbishop visit.** (pg 113)

15 Sep 1850 – **Manuel Rafael Martines**, resident of el Rito, widower of 1st marriage to Mariana Sanches, deceased, resident of Casita, m. **Juana Maria Atencio**, resident of el Rito, legit d/ Ylario Atencio, deceased, and Maria Paula Torres. (pg 113b)

23 Sep 1850 – **Francisco Atencio**, resident of Ojo Caliente, legit s/ Pedro Atencio, deceased and Maria de Jesus Aguilar, residents of Ojo Caliente, m. **Maria de la Lus Sisneros**, resident of the same place, legit d/ Jose Gabriel Sisneros, deceased, and Maria Brigida Duran; pad/ Jose Antonio Trugillo and Maria Rita Baca, residents of the same place. (pg 113b/114)

23 Sep 1850 – **Francisco Antonio Salasar**, resident of los Cañones, legit s/ Juan Salasar and Gertrudis Suaso, residents of los Cañones, m. **Maria Antonia Valdes**, resident of the same place, legit d/ Pedro Ygnacio Valdes and Mariana Josefa Gonsales; pad/ Jose Pablo Abeyta and Maria Rosa Salasar; wit/ Pablo Abeyta and Rafael Gallegos. (pg 114)

23 Sep 1850 – **Juan Andres Quintana**, resident of Abiquiu, legit s/ Miguel Quintana, deceased, and Maria Teodora Sisneros, m. **Maria Delubina Salasar**, resident of Abiquiu, legit d/ Pedro Salasar and Acencion Vigil; pad/ Pablo Trugillo and Maria Reyes Vigil; wit/ Pablo Abeyta and Sabino Salasar. (pg 114b)

26 Sep 1850 – **Juan Agustin Basques**, resident of Abiquiu, legit s/ Agustin Basques and Maria de la Lus Martines, residents of Abiquiu, m. **Maria Tomasa Abila**, resident of el Rito, legit d/ Domingo Abila and Maria Manuela Olibas; wit/ Pablo Abeyta and Juan Agustin Chaves. (pg 114b/115)

29 Oct 1850 – **Juan Santos Torres**, resident of el Rito, legit s/ Bernardo Torres and Maria Gertrudis Jaques, residents of la Cueva, m. **Maria Catalina Archuleta**, resident of el Rito, legit d/ Jose Miguel Archuleta and Maria Isabel Casados; pad/ Jesus Maria Lucero and Maria Lucia Valdes, residents of the same place; wit/ Jose Maria Montaño and Fernando Montaño. (pg 115)

30 Oct 1850 – **Juan Jose Gallegos**, resident of Ojo Caliente, widower of 1st marriage to Maria Paula Gomes, deceased, m. **Maria Asencion Jaramillo**, resident of Ojo Caliente, legit d/ Diego Antonio Jaramillo and Maria Antonia Lucero, deceased; pad/ Miguel Martin and Maria Francisca Ruibal, residents of the same place; wit/ Salbador Lucero and Vicente Jaramillo. (pg 115/115b)

6 Nov 1850 – **Antonio Jose Domingues**, legit s/ Jose Domingues and Maria Manuela Martines, deceased, residents of Ojo Caliente, m. **Maria Ruperta Espinosa**, resident of this church, legit d/ Julian Espinosa and Maria Juliana Rubali; wit/ Jose Maria Montaño and Julian Ocaña. (pg 115b)

6 Nov 1850 – **Jose Tomas de Aquino Archuleta**, legit s/ Nicolas Archuleta, deceased, and Maria Gertrudis Alire, residents of los Ancones, m. **Maria Juana Rosalia Martines**, resident of Questa, natural d/ Maria Victoria Martines; pad/ Antonio Domingo Lucero and Maria Rugina Valdes; wit/ Jose Maria Martin and Juan Olguin. (pg 115b)

11 Nov 1850 – **Manuel Antonio Torres**, resident of Ojo Caliente, legit s/ Carlos Torres and Maria Josefa Valdes, residents of Ojo Caliente, m. **Maria Manuela Peña**, resident of the same place, legit d/ Rafael Peña and Maria de la Crus Trugillo; wit/ Jose Manuel Vigil and Jose Maria Montaño. (pg 116)

15 Nov 1850 – **Faustin Trugillo**, widower of Maria Gertrudis Mansanares, m. **Maria Loreta Apodaca**, resident of el Rito, natural d/ Juana Maria Apodaca; pad/ Jose Francisco Trugillo and Maria Ruperta Armijo; wit/ Jose Maria Montaño and Fernando Montaño. (pg 116/116b)

15 Nov 1850 – **Antonio Lino Lopes**, legit s/ Ramon Lopes and Maria Lugarda Espinosa, m. **Maria Manuela Ribera**, resident of the same place, natural d/ Maria Dolores Ribera; wit/ Jose Maria Montaño and
Quirino Ocaña. (pg 116b)

15 Nov 1850 – **Rafael Jaques**, resident of Ojo Caliente, legit s/ Juan de Jesus Jaques, deceased, and Maria Juana Trugillo, residents of Ojo Caliente, m. **Maria Josefa Valdes**, resident of Ojo Caliente, legit d/ Antonio Nerio Valdes and Maria Josefa Valdes; wit/ Pablo Abeyta and Antonio Ortis. (pg 116b/117)

17 Nov 1850 – **Fernandes Martines**, resident of Ojo Caliente, legit s/ Juan del Rosario Martines and Maria Josefa Mansanares, resident, m. **Maria Miquela Maes**, resident of the same place, legit d/ Juan Manuel Maes and Maria Polonia Jiron; wit/ Jose Manuel Martin and Juan Olguin. (pg 117)

30 Nov 1850 – **Jose Manuel Madrid**, resident of Tierra Azul, legit s/ Miguel Antono Madrid and Maria Josefa Duran, residents of Tierra Azul, m. **Maria Josefa Chaves**, widow of 1st marriage to Eusebio Martin; pad/ Julian Martines and Maria del Refugio Martines; wit/ Jose Pablo Abeyta and Juan Leonor Abeyta. (pg 117/117b)

4 Dec 1850 – **Jose Andres Martines**, resident of Ojo Caliente, legit s/ Ramon Martines and Maria Clara Mestas, residents of la Casita, m. **Maria Josefa Trujillo**, resident of Ojo Caliente, legit d/ Jose Miguel Trugillo and Maria Rufina Espinosa; pad/ Sabino Salasar and Maria Justafina Lopes; wit/ Jose Manuel Montaño and Diego Madrid. (pg 117b)

8 Dec 1850 – **Jose Miguel Trugillo**, resident of la Cueva, legit s/ Jose Maria Trugillo and Maria Marcelina Ruivibali, deceased, residents of Abiquiu, m. **Maria Juliana Atencio**, resident of la Cueva, legit d/ Francisco Antonio Atencio and Maria Dolores Martines; pad/ Andres Trugillo and Maria Estefana Valdes, residents of los Ancones; wit/ Jose Maria Montaño and Fernando Montaño. (pg no #)

17 Dec 1850 – **Silberio Valdes**, resident of Ojo Caliente, legit s/ Mariano Valdes, deceased, and Maria Manuela Maes, residents of Ojo Caliente, m. **Maria Juana Martines**, resident of the same place, legit d/ Jose Julian Martines and Maria Ygnes Martin; pad/ Antonio Domingo Lucero and Maria Rufina Valdes, residents of Ojo Caliente; wit/ Jose Manuel Martin and Juan Olguin. (pg no #/no #b)

18 Dec 1850 – **Pedro Antonio de Herrera**, resident of Ojo Caliente, legit s/ Jose Miguel de Herrera and Maria Rita Bargas, residents of the parish of San Juan, m. **Maria Martina Maes**, resident of Ojo Caliente, legit d/ Juan Manuel Maes and Maria Polonia Giron; pad/ Felipe Casias and Bibiana Lucero, residents of el Rito; wit/ Jose Maria Montaño and Miguel Gallegos. (pg 118b)

21 Dec 1850 – **Pedro Antonio de Esquipula Ortega**, resident of el Rito, legit s/ Juan Ortega and Maria Paula Chaves, deceased, residents of el Rito, m. **Maria Manuela Alire**, resident of the same place, legit d/ Santiago Alire and Maria Natividad Garcia; pad/ Felipe Casias and Maria Biviana Lucero; wit/ Jose Maria Montaño and Fernando Montaño. (pg no #/118)

28 Dec 1850 – **Jose Francisco Trujillo**, resident of Abiquiu, widower of Maria Ygnacia Valdes, m. **Maria Antonia Alire**, resident of Ojo Caliente, legit d/ Jose Manuel Alire and Maria Dolores Maes; pad/ Jose Tomas Montaño and Maria Rosa del Pilar Montaño, residents of el Rito. (pg 118/118b)

28 Dec 1850 – **Jose Deciderio Lobato**, resident of el Rito, legit s/ Baltasar Lobato and Maria Victoria Mestas, residents of el Rito, m. **Maria Leonor Sanches**, resident of el Rito, legit d/ Juan Andres Sanches, deceased, and Maria de la Lus Lucero; pad/ Antonio Ortega and Maria de la Lus Valdes, residents of the same place; wit/ Jose Manuel Vigil and Jose Ramon Sisneros. (pg 118b)

1 Jan 1851 – **Jose Francisco Gonsales**, resident of Abquiu, legit s/ Salbador Gonsales and Maria Tomasa Sisneros, residents of Abiquiu, m. **Maria Dolores Martines**, resident of the same place, widow; pad/ Antonio Ortega and Maria de la Luz Valdes; wit/ Jose Tomas Romero and Salbador Mansanares. (pg 118b/119)

5 Jan 1851 – **Jose Maria Maes**, resident of Abiquiu, legit s/ Pedro Maes, deceased, and Maria Gertrudis Duran, deceased, m. **Maria del Refugio Alarid**, resident of Abiquiu, legit d/ Juan Andres Alarid and Maria Dorotea Aragon, deceased; pad/ Antonio Maria Salas and Roberta Lobato, residents of Ojo Caliente; wit/ Jose Tomas Romero and Salbador Mansanares. (pg 119)

6 Jan 1851 – **Juan Andres Chaves**, resident of Abiquiu, legit s/ Juan Agustin Chaves and Maria Juana Martin, residents of Abiquiu, m. **Maria Josefa Martin**, resident of the same place, widow of Noberto Chacon, deceased; wit/ Jose Manuel Gallegos and Refugio Montoya. (pg 119/119b)

12 Jan 1851 – **Manuel Gregorio Trujillo**, resident of Abiquiu, legit s/ Francisco Estevan Trujillo, deceased, and Maria Loreta Martin, m. **Maria Ygnacia Salasar**, resident of Abquiu, legit d/ Sebastian Salasar and Maria Victoria del Castillo; pad/ Andres Salasar and Soledad Salasar; wit/ Juan Agustin Chaves and Geronimo Gallegos. (pg 119b)

12 Jan 1851 – **Manuel Antonio Romero**, resident of Ojo Caliente, legit s/ Jose Miguel Romero and Maria Serafina Sandobal, residents of Ojo Caliente, m. **Maria Rosa Martines**, resident of the same place, legit d/ Jose Maria Martines, deceased, and Maria Juana Lucero; pad/ Antonio Maria Salas and Roberta Lobato, residents of Ojo Caliente; wit/ Ramon Cordoba and Geronimo Jaramillo. (pg 120)

27 Mar 1851 – **Diego Antonio Martines**, resident of Abliquiu, legit s/ Pedro Antonio Martines, deceased, and Maria Paula Manchego, m. **Maria Trinidad Belasques**, resident of Abiquiu, widow of Juan Antonio Gallegos; pad/ Juan Agustin Chaves and Maria Juana Martin, residents of Abiquiu; wit/ Jose Manuel Gallegos and Refugio Montoya. (pg 120)

29 Mar 1851 – **Jose Pablo Martines**, resident of Ojo Caliente, legit s/ Jose Manuel Martines and Maria Rita Villalpando, m. **Maria Natividad Sanches**, resident of Ojo Caliente, legit d/ Ramos Sanches, deceased, and Maria Leonisia Lobato; pad/ Antonio Maria Salas and Roberta Lobato, residents of Ojo Caliente; wit/ Manuel Chacon and Antonio Jose Mora. (pg 120b)

20 Jan 1851 – **Juan Esteban Trujillo**, resident of Abiquiu, legit s/ Ysidro Trujillo, deceased, and Maria de la Luz Garcia, m. **Maria de la Luz Trujillo**, resident of Abiquiu, legit d/ Jose Manuel Trujillo, deceased, and Maria Mauricia Martin; pad/ Juan Pascual Martin and Ysidora Garcia, resident of the same place; wit/ Geronimo Gallegos and Esteban Benavides. (pg 120b/121)

25 Jan 1851 – **Quirino Belasques**, resident of Abiquiu, legit s/ Jose Joaquin Belasques, deceased, and Antonia Rosa Romero, m. **Maria Catarina Salasar**, resident of Abiquiu, legit d/ Juan Salasar and Maria Gertrudis Sena; pad/ Juan Agustin Chaves and Maria Juana Martin, residents of Abiquiu; wit/ Guadalupe Gallegos and Francisco Chaves. (pg 121)

25 Jan 1851 – **Jose Andres Duran**, legit s/ Diego Duran, deceased, and Maria de la Luz Marques, m. **Maria Dolores Salasar**, resident of los Cañones, widow of Juan Antonio Sisneros, deceased; pad/ Crecencio Duran and Maria Juana Quintana; wit/ Pedro Sandobal and Juan Martin. (pg 121/121b)

25 Jan 1851 – **Juan Lente**, legit s/ Manuel Lente, deceased, and Maria Rafaela Gallegos, m. **Maria Juana Vigil**, resident of Abiquiu, legit d/ Faustin Vigil, deceased, and Maria Manuela Jaramillo; pad/ Bartolo Mestas and Candelaria Sisneros; wit/ Rafael Valdes and Pedro Abeyta. (pg 121b)

9 Feb 1851 – **Juan de Jesus Mestas**, legit s/ Rafael Mestas, deceased, and Maria de la Lus Mascareñas, m. **Maria Seferina Martines**, resident of Tierra Azul, legit d/ Albino Martines and Maria Altagracia Quintana; pad/ Rafael Vigil and Natividad Sanches; wit/ Pablo Quintana and Pedro Duran. (pg 121/122)

23 Feb 1851 – **Diego Rodrigues**, legit s/ Diego Rodrigues, deceased, and Maria Gregoria Vijil, m. **Maria Candelaria Ruis**, resident of Ojo Caliente, legit d/ Rafael Ruis, deceased, and Maria Antonia Martin; pad/ Jose Manuel Vijil and Estefana Gonsales; wit/ Pedro Garcia and Francisco Chacon. (pg 122)

23 Feb 1851 – **Jose Antonio Lopes**, servant of Miguel Lopes and Maria Manuela Mestas, m. **Maria Paula Lopes**, resident of this parish, legit d/ Juan Cristobal Lopes and Maria Manuela Chaves; pad/ Pedro de Herrera and Nicolasa Martin; wit/ Pedro Salas and Juan Torres. (pg 122/122b)

23 Feb 1851 – **Cleto Trujillo**, legit s/ Pedro Trujillo and Maria Antonia Sanches, deceased, m. **Maria Guadalupe Abeyta**, resident of Abiquiu, legit d/ Juan de Jesus Abeyta, deceased, and Maria Loreta Trujillo; pad/ Cristobal Martin and Josefa Torres; wit/ Pedro Lujan and Jose Pablo Trujillo. (pg 122b)

26 Mar 1851 – **Francisco Antonio Martines**, adopted s/ Ysidro Pancario Martines and Maria de las Niebes Coca, m. **Maria Ysidora Chaves**, resident of Abiquiu, legit d/ Juan Agustin Chaves and Maria Juana Gertrudis Martin; pad/ Francisco Esteban Chaves and Maria del Jesus Montaño; wit/ Pedro Leon Lujan and Jose Pablo Trujillo. (pg 122b/123)

26 Mar 1851 – **Agapito Martin**, widower of Rufina Salasar, deceased, m. **Maria Agustina Jaques**, resident of Ojo Caliente, legit d/ Felipe Jaques and Maria Micaela Chaves; pad/ Clemente Trujillo and Brigida Quintana; wit/ Diego Ortega and Ramon Martin. (pg 123)

4 Apr 1851 – **Jose Aniseto Martin**, legit s/ Julian Martin and Maria Ygnes Martin, m. **Maria Josefa Madrid**, resident of Ojo Caliente, legit d/ Jose Rafael Madrid and Maria Faustina Lucero; pad/ Pablo Garcia and Teodora Apodaca; wit/ Julian Martin and Juan Agustin Chaves. (pg 123b)

8 Jun 1851 – **Jose Maria Jiron**, legit s/ Juan Emilio Jiron, deceased, and Maria del Carmen Galbis, m. **Maria Felisiana Gonsales**, resident of el Rito, legit d/ Jose Maria Gonsales and Maria Ygnacia Martines; pad/ Bautista Vigil and Candelaria Maes; wit/ Guadalupe Gallegos and Geronimo Gallegos. (pg 123b)

15 Jun 1851 – **Guadalupe Gallegos**, widower of Maria Barbara Trujillo, m. **Maria Francisca Gutierres**, resident of Abiquiu, legit d/ Jose Antonio Gutierres, deceased, and Maria Ygnacia Trujillo; pad/ Geronimo Gallegos and Juana Duran; wit/ Pedro Lura Lujan and Pablo Trujillo. (pg 123b/124)

3 Aug 1851 – **Vicente Chaves**, legit s/ Marcos Chaves, deceased, and Maria Dolores Garcia, m. **Maria Margarita Martin**, resident of Abiquiu, widow of Juan Salasar, deceased; pad/ Juan Agustin Chaves and Juana Martin; wit/ Jose Pablo Trujillo and Pedro Antonio Martines. (pg 124)

27 Sep 1851 – **Jose Antonio Trujillo**, legit s/ Salbador Trujillo and Maria Rita Baca, m. **Maria Aniseta Martin**, resident of Ojo Caliente, legit d/ Seferino Martin and Juana Catarina Valdes; pad/ Blas Trujillo and Consepcion Salasar, residents of Chamita; wit/ Jose Pablo Abeyta and Rafael Valdes. (pg 124/124b)

12 Oct 1851 – **Jose Teodoro Gurule**, widower of Maria Juliana Baca, m. **Maria Rufina Lucero**, resident of el Rito, legit d/ Pablo Lucero and Guadalupe Ribera; pad/ Juan Gurule and Maria Clara Baca; wit/ Francisco Vigil and Jose Antonio Armijo. (pg 124 b)

24 Oct 1851 – **Francisco Antonio Martin**, legit s/ Jose Manuel Martin and Maria Juana Valdes, m. **Maria Candelaria Mestas**, resident of Ojo Caliente, legit d/ Miguel Mestas and Josefa Samora; pad/ Miguel Martin and Francisca Gallegos; wit/ Salbador Lucero and Juan Olguin. (pg 124b/125)

1 Nov 1851 – **Jose Maria Lucero**, legit s/ Gregorio Lucero and Maria Antonia Lujan, m. **Maria de la Lus Chaves**, resident of the Casitas, legit d/ Julian Chaves and Maria Josefa Martines; pad/ Francisco Martin and Candelaria Mestas; wit/ Ramon Martin and Pedro Abeyta. (pg 125)

12 Nov 1851 – **Jose Teodoro Martin**, legit s/ Baltsar Martin and Guadalupe Martin, m. **Maria Serafina Vigil**, resident of la Casita, legit d/ Pedro Vigil, deceased, and Maria Ygnacia Lara; pad/ Juan de Jesus Lucero and Maria Soledad <u>Forangas</u>; wit/ Juan Jose Gallegos and Geronimo Jaramillo. (pg 125)

12 Nov 1851 – **Jose Gabriel Gallegos**, legit s/ Santiago Gallegos and Viatris Sandobal, deceased, m. **Maria Rafaela Martin**, resident of Ojo Caliente, legit d/ Jesus Maria Martin and Maria Rosalia Trujillo; pad/ Rafael Fresquis and Maria Garcia; wit/ Antonio Valdes and Prudencio Gonsales. (pg 125b)

28 Nov 1851 – **Jose Eusebio Valdes**, widower of Maria Manuela Martines, m. **Maria Consepcion Trujillo**, widow of 1st marriage to Jose Muños; pad/ Pablo Salasar and Francisca Molina. (pg 125b)

28 Nov 1851 – **Juan de Dios Ruibal**, legit s/ Antonio Ruibal, deceased, and Ana Maria Chaves, deceased, m. **Maria de Jesus Esquipula Jaramillo**, resident of Ojo Caliente, legit d/ Jose Miguel Jaramillo and Maria Manuela Martin, deceased; pad/ Juan Jose Gallegos and Maria Acencion Jaramillo; wit/ Jose de la Cruz Padilla and Clemente Sandobal. (pg 125b/126)

28 Nov 1851 – **Pedro Antonio Garcia**, natural s/ Guadalupe Garcia, m. **Maria Teodora Martin**, resident of Abiquiu, legit d/ Jose Antonio Martin and Maria Rutila Mestas; pad/ Juan Nepomuceno Valdes and Maria Juana Archuleta; wit/ Diego de Luna and Martin Trujillo. (pg 126)

10 Dec 1851 – **Candelario Lobato**, legit s/ Antonio Lobato and Maria Dolores Chacon, m. **Maria Soledad Martin**, resident of los Ancones, legit d/ Juan Manuel Martin and Consepcion Lucero; pad/ Juan Gabriel Chacon and Maria de la Lus Belasques; wit/ Manuel Gallegos and Antonio Jaramillo. (pg 126/126b)

13 Dec 1851 – **Jesus Maria Martines**, legit s/ Jose Francisco Martin and Maria Pascuala Jiron, deceased, m. **Maria Guadalupe Martin**, resident of el Rito, legit d/ Pedro Martin and Maria Ygnes Trujillo; pad/ Juan Gabriel Chacon and Maria de la Lus Belasques; wit/ Pedro Gomes and Pedro Espinosa. (pg 126b)

27 Dec 1851 – **Eugenio Jaramillo**, legit s/ Pedro Jaramillo and Ygnacia Olguin, m. **Maria Juana Martin**, resident of Abiquiu, legit d/ Felipe Martin, deceased, and Biviana Trujillo; pad/ Pedro Trujillo and Altagracia Martin; wit/ Pablo Duran and Juan Martin. (pg 126b/127)

27 Dec 1851 – **Antonio Bibian Maes**, legit s/ Gabriel Maes, deceased, and Barbara Baca, deceased, m. **Maria Petra Pando**, resident of Ojo Caliente, legit d/ Candelario Pando, deceased, and Carmen Martines; pad/ Simon Martin and Juana Maria Trujillo; wit/ Miguel Martin and Reyes Rodrigues. (pg 127)

27 Dec 1851 – **Juan de la Cruz Espinosa**, legit s/ Francisco Espinosa, deceased, and Maria Antonia Quintana, m. **Maria Agapita Valdes**, resident of el Rito, legit d/ German Valdes, deceased, and Josefa Gomes, deceased; pad/ Juan Gurule and Maria Clara Baca; wit/ Francisco Vigil and Jose Antonio Armijo. (pg 127)

27 Dec 1851 – **Jose Albino Baca**, widower of Maria Gertrudis Cabesa de Baca, deceased, m. **Maria Dolores Gallegos**, resident of Abiquiu, legit d/ Miguel Antonio Gallegos and Rumalda Lucero; pad/ Antonio Jose Ribera and Maria Barbara Gallegos; wit/ Jose Manuel Valdes and Pedro Leon Lujan. (pg 127b)

27 Dec 1851 – **Bernabel Gallegos**, natural s/ Maria Dolores Benabides, m. **Maria de la Cruz Trujillo**, single legit d/ Ysidro Trujillo, deceased, and Maria Tomasa Romero; pad/ Rafael Ocana and Maria de Jesus Martin; wit/ Pablo Trujillo and Geronimo Gallegos. (pg 127b)

27 Dec 1851 – **Bernardo Trujillo**, legit s/ Jose Manuel Trujillo and Maria Mauricia Martin, m. **Maria Rita Gallegos**, resident of the Pueblo, legit d/ Manuel Gallegos and Ana Maria Ulibarri; pad/ Antonio Mansanares and Maria Rafela Mansanares; wit/ Pedro Salasar and Francisco Martin. (pg 128)

27 Dec 1851 – **Jesus Maria Salasar**, legit s/ Santiago Salasar and Maria Dolores Romero, m. **Maria Rosalia Archuleta**, resident of Abiquiu, legit d/ Jose Antonio Archuleta and Maria Juana Mansanares; pad/ Rafael Ocana and Juana Maria Martin; wit/ Pedro Trujillo and Jose Maria Trujillo. (pg 128)

18 Jan 1852 – **Juan Antonio Lopes**, natural s/ Maria Manuela Lopes, m. **Maria Guadalupe Montaño**, resident of Abiquiu, legit d/ Fernando Montaño and Maria de Jesus Delgado; pad/ Jose de la Lus Gallegos and Maria Carmelia Gallegos. (pg 128b)

28 Dec 1852 – **Jose Albino Trugillo**, single legit s/ Jose Maria Trugillo and Mauricia Martines, m. **Maria Gracia Gutierres**, resident of the Pueblo, legit d/ Juaquin Gutierres, deceased, and Juana Catarina Gonsales; wit/ Jose Santiago Trugillo and Juan Agustin Chavez. (pg 129)

28 Dec 1852 – **Jose Francisco Trugillo**, resident of Ojo Caliente, legit s/ Jose Trugillo, deceased, and Maria Equipula Valdes, m. **Maria Gregoria Salas**, resident of el Rito, legit d/

Diego Salas, deceased, and Maria Manuela Espinoza; wit/ Juan Jose Espinosa and Reyes Martinez. (pg 129/129b)

28 Dec 1852 – **Bernardo Garcia**, legit s/ Jose Maria Garcia and Maria Manuela Coris, m. **Natividad Jaramillo**, all residents of the Pueblo, legit d/ Ramon Jaramillo, deceased, and Maria Teodora Martinez; wit/ Geronimo Gallegos and Pedro Ygnacio NS. (pg 129b)

1 Jan 1853 – **Jose Domingo Salasar**, natural s/ Juana Salasar, m. **Maria Natividad Belasques**, resident of the Pueblo, legit d/ Ygnacio Belasques and Maria Manuela Gonsales, deceased; wit/ Santiago Trugillo and Jose Rafael Duran. (pg 129b/130)

1 Jan 1853 – **Jose Manuel de Jesus Archuleta**, legit s/ Francisco Archuleta and Maria Barbara Lopes, residents of Abiquiu, m. **Maria Ruperta Gomes**, resident of el Rito, legit d/ Jose Pedro Gomes and Maria Manuela Martines; wit/ Juan Agustin Chaves and Jose Ygnacio Valdes. (pg 130)

1 Jan 1853 – **Antonio Matias Velasques**, legit s/ Ygnacio Velasques and Manuela Gonsales, deceased, m. **Maria Alta Gracia Valdes**, resident of los Cañones, legit d/ Pedro Antonio Valdes and Maria Consepcion Garcia; wit/ Santiago Trugillo and Jose Rafael Duran. (pg 130/130b)

1 Jan 1853 – **Mariano Gallegos**, legit s/ Roman Gallegos, deceased, and Maria Dolores Castillo, residents of Abiquiu, m. **Maria Manuela Velasquez**, resident of Abiquiu, legit d/ Ygnacio Velasquez and Maria Manuela Gonsales, deceased; wit/ Santiago Trugillo and Jose Rafael Martines. (pg 130b)

1 Jan 1853 – **Juan Rafael Madril**, legit s/ Cristobal Madril and Maria Josefa Moya, residents of los Cañones, m. **Maria Paubla Trugillo**, resident of Abiquiu, legit d/ Francisco Antonio Trugillo and Maria Josefa Trugillo, deceased; wit/ Santiago Trugillo and Juan Agustin Chaves. (pg 130b/131)

1 Jan 1853 – **Antonio Jose Martines**, legit s/ Cristobal Martines and Josefa Alarid, residents of La Bega, m. **Maria Ynes Martines**, resident of Abiquiu, legit d/ Francisco Martines and Encarnacion Garcia; wit/ Santiago Trugillo and Jose Rafael Duran. (pg 131)

1 Jan 1853 – **Jose de Jesus Martines**, legit s/ Juan Jose Martines and Ines Madrid, residents of el Rito, m. **Ysavel Madrid**, single legit d/ Miguel Madrid, deceased, and Encarnacion Martines; wit/ Santiago Trugillo and Jose Rafael Duran. (pg 131/131b)

6 Jan 1853 – **Tomas Archuleta**, resident of Ojo Caliente, widower of Juana Martines, deceased, m. **Maria Guadalupe Marques**, resident of the same place, legit d/ Vicente Marques and Getrudis Chacon, deceased; wit/ Jesus Maria Varela and Jose Manuel Martines. (pg 131b)

6 Jan 1853 – **Hermenegildo Martines**, legit s/ Juan Manuel Martines and Maria Concepcion Lucero, residents of Ojo Caliente, m. **Maria Antonia Trugillo**, resident of la Cueva, natural d/ Maria Manuela Trugillo, deceased; wit/ Jesus Maria Varela and Jose Manuel Martines. (pg 131b)

6 Jan 1853 – **Antonio Maes**, legit s/ Santiago Maes, deceased, and Reyes Martines, deceased, residents of Ojo Caliente, m. **Maria Josefa Gallegos**, resident of the same place, legit d/ Jose Miguel Gallegos and Margarita Lucero, deceased; wit/ Jesus Maria Varela and Jose Manuel Martines. (pg 131b/132)

6 Jan 1853 – **Jose Antonio Archuleta**, legit s/ Manuel Archuleta, deceased, and Maria Getrudis Trugillo, residents of Ojo Caliente, m. **Juana Maria Rodrigues**, resident of the same place, legit d/ Francisco Rodrigues and Maria Rosa Salas, deceased; wit/ Jose Maria Varela and Jose Manuel Martines. (pg 132)

6 Jan 1853 – **Juan de Luna**, legit s/ Pablo de Luna, deceased, and Maria Guadalupe Lucero, residents of Ojo Caliente, m. **Ana Maria Sandobal**, resident of Taos, legit d/ Salbador Sandobal, deceased, and Juana Maria Alarid; wit/ Jesus Maria Varela and Jose Manuel Martines. (pg 132)

6 Jan 1853 – **Francisco Gonsales**, legit s/ Pablo Gonsales and Paubla Atencio, deceased, residents of San Juan Nepomuceno of el Rito, m. **Maria Trinidad Garcia**, resident of the same place, natural d/ Nicolasa Garcia, deceased; wit/ Julian Alire and Juan Manuel Gallego. (pg 132b)

30 Jan 1853 – **Jesus Merced Valdes**, legit s/ Simon Valdes and Maria de la Lus Quintana, residents of San Juan Nepomuceno of el Rito, m. **Maria Ygnacia Valdes**, resident of Chama, legit d/ Francisco Valdes, deceased, and Nicolasa Romo; wit/ Cruz Lujan and Agustin Gallegos. (pg 132b)

30 Jan 1853 – **Juan Ysidro Gallegos**, legit s/ Domingo Gallegos and Maria Concepcion Velasques, deceased, residents of el Rito, m. **Maria Natividad Garcia**, resident of the same place, natural d/ Maria Trinidad Garcia; wit/ Julian Alire and Juan Manuel Gallegos. (pg 132b/133)

30 Jan 1853 – **Jose Deciderio Martines**, legit s/ Juan Antonio Martines and Maria Ygnacia Valdes, residents of el Rito, m. **Maria Dolores Trugillo**, resident of the same place, legit d/ Jose Ramon Trugillo and Maria Paubla Roibal; wit/ Julian Alire and Juan Manuel Gallegos. (pg 133)

30 Jan 1853 – **Juan de Jesus Alire**, legit s/ Miguel Alire and Dolores Gallegos, residents of Ojo Caliente, m. **Maria Soledad Samora**, resident of Ojo Caliente, legit d/ Miguel Samora, deceased, and Maria Manuela Valdes; wit/ Jesus Maria Varela and Jose Manuel Martines. (pg 133)

30 Jan 1853 – **Luis Ocaña**, legit s/ Julian Ocaña and Maria de la Lus Valdes, deceased, residents of el Rito, m. **Maria Josefa Gallegos**, resident of the same place, legit d/ Miguel Gallegos, deceased, and Ysavel Sandoval; wit/ Santiago Trugillo and Pablo Abeyta. (pg 133)

6 Feb 1853 – **Juan de Jesus Martines**, widower of Maria Gertrudes Lucero, deceased, residents of Taos, m. **Maria Matiana Archuleta**, resident of San Antonio de la Servilleta, legit d/ Jose Miguel Archuleta and Ysavel Venavides, deceased; wit/ Jesus Maria Barela and Jose Manuel Martines. (pg 133b)

13 Feb 1853 – **Jose Merced Trugillo**, legit s/ Jose Ysidro Trugillo, deceased, and Ana Maria Martines, residents of San Jose de Chama, m. **Maria Sipriana Gallegos**, resident of the same place, legit d/ Eulogio Gallegos and Maria del Refugio Valdes; wit/ Jesus Maria Varela and Jose Manuel Martines. (pg 133b)

17 Feb 1853 – **Pedro Antonio de Herrera**, widower of Getrudes Trugillo, deceased, residents of el Rito, m. **Maria Francisca Ocaña**, resident of the same place, legit d/ Julian Ocaña and Maria de la Luz Valdes, deceased; wit/ Julian Alire and Juan Manuel Gallegos. (pg 133b)

17 Feb 1853 – **Juan Nepomuceno Archuleta**, legit s/ Manuel Archuleta, deceased, and Maria Getrudis Trugillo, residents of Ojo Caliente, m. **Maria Rosalia Vargas**, resident of San Juan, legit d/ Jose Vargas and Maria del Rosario Sisneros; wit/ Jesus Maria Varela and Jose Manuel Martines. (pg 134)

17 Feb 1853 – **Jose Antonio Garcia**, legit s/ Jose Pablo Garcia, deceased, and Maria Getrudis Abeyta, residents of San Jose del Barranca, m. **Maria Rufina Salasar**, resident of the same place, legit d/ Esquipula Salasar and Maria Francisca Serrano; wit/ Santiago Trugillo and Pablo Abeyta. (pg 134)

13 Mar 1853 – **Vicente Lujan**, natural s/ Maria Dolores Lujan, residents of el Rito, m. **Maria Rafaela Martines**, resident of the same place, legit d/ Juan Miguel Martines and Maria Candelaria Espinosa, deceased; wit/ Julian Alire and Bitero Archuleta. (pg 134)

20 Mar 1853 – **Juan de Dios Martines**, legit s/ Jose Manuel Martines and Maria Rita Vialpando, resident of la Cueba, m. **Maria Josefa <u>Ruibali</u>, resident** of the same place, legit d/ Juan

Ulibarri, deceased, and Josefa Garcia; wit/ Jesus Maria Varela and Jose Manuel Martines. (pg 134b)

24 Apr 1853 – **Antonio Valdes**, legit s/ Jose Manuel Valdes and Maria Paubla Ruibali, residents of the pueblo of Abiquiu, m. **Maria Concepcion Garcia**, resident of the same place, legit d/ Mariano Garcia and Maria de la Lus Chaves; wit/ Santiago Trugillo and Pablo Abeyta. (pg 134b)

24 Apr 1853 – **Francisco Antonio Archuleta**, legit s/ Candelario Archuleta and Maria Dolores Lucero, deceased, residents of Ojo Caliente, m. **Juana Teresa de Jesus Maes**, resident of Ojo Caliente, legit d/ Juan Manuel Maes, deceased, and Maria Polonia Giron; wit/ Jesus Maria Varela and Jose Manuel Martines. (pg 134b)

8 May 1853 – **Jose Francisco Martines**, legit s/ Nicolas Martines and Guadalupe Valdes, residents of Servilleta, m. **Maria del Rosario Chaves**, resident of the same place, widow of 1st marriage to Bitor Cordoba, deceased; wit/ Jesus Maria Varela and Jose Manuel Martines. (pg 135)

8 May 1853 – **Juan de Jesus Duran**, legit s/ Yisdro Duran and Maria Soledad de Herrera, residents of Ojo Caliente, m. **Maria Andrea Velasques**, resident of the same place, legit d/ Mateo Velasques, deceased, and Maria Arcadia Montoya; wit/ Jesus Maria Varela and Jose Manuel Martines. (pg 135)

26 May 1853 – **Jose Gregorio Vigil,** servant of Jose Francisco Vigil, deceased, and Maria Dolores Lopes, deceased, residents of Abiquiu, m. **Maria Manuela Velasques**, resident of Abiquiu, legit d/ Jose Velasques, deceased, and Maria Monica Martines; wit/ Santiago Trugillo and Pablo Abeyta. (pg 135)

26 May 1853 – **Jose Fernando Montaño**, legit s/ Jose Maria Montaño and Antonia Getrudis Quintana, residents of el Rito, m. **Maria Josefa Jaramillo**, resident of Ojo Caliente, legit d/ Diego Antonio Jaramillo and Maria Antonia Lucero; wit/ Jesus Maria Varela and Jose Manuel Martines. (pg 135b)

26 May 1853 – **Jose Cortes**, legit s/ Jose Cortes and Rosalia Dolores NS, residents of Canada, m. **Maria Bartola Mestas**, resident of San Antonio of Valle, legit d/ Carmen Mestas; wit/ Jesus Maria Varela and Jose Manuel Martines. (pg 135b)

21 Aug 1853 – **Jose Dolores Duran**, widower of Maria Manuela Martines, deceased, residents of el Rito, m. **Maria Ines Urtado**, resident of the same place, legit d/ Antonio Nerio Urtado and Maria Ramona Guillen; wit/ Santiago Trugillo and Pablo Abeyta. (pg 135b)

28 Aug 1853 – **Juan Nepomuceno Medina**, legit s/ Ygnacio Medina and Maria Martines, residents of Ojo Caliente, m. **Maria de la Lus Salas**, resident of the same place, natural d/ Maria Juana Salas, deceased; wit/ Jesus Maria Varela and Jose Manuel Martines. (pg 136)

18 Sep 1853 – **Juan Bautista Jaques**, legit s/ Felipe Jaques, deceased, and Maria Miguela Chaves, deceased, residents of Ojo Caliente, m. **Maria Simona Martines**, resident of the same place, legit d/ Juan Manuel Martines and Maria Concepcion Lucero; wit/ Julian Alire and Bitervo Archuleta. (pg 136)

25 Sep 1853 – **Jose Manuel Vigil**, legit s/ Juan Angel Vigil, deceased, and Maria Guadalupe Vallejo, residents of Arroyo Hondo, m. **Maria Ramona Vigil**, resident of Ojo Caliente, legit d/ Jose Manuel Vigil and Esquipula Quintana; wit/ Julian Alire and Bisensio Archuleta. (pg 136)

25 Sep 1853 – **Manuel de Jesus Archuleta**, legit s/ Francisco Archuleta, deceased, and Maria Getrudes Alire, residents of Ojo Caliente, m. **Maria Estefana de Herrera**, resident of Ojo Caliente, legit d/ Juan de Jesus de Herrera, deceased, and Maria Rufina Valdes; wit/ Jesus Maria Varela and Jose Manuel Martines. (pg 136b)

2 Oct 1853 – **Jose Venedito Lucero**, legit s/ Juan del Carmen Lucero and Maria Rosa Martines, deceased, residents of el Rito, m. **Maria Juana Trugillo**, resident of the same place, legit d/ Juan Rafael Trugillo and Maria Rosalia Atencio; wit/ Julian Alire and Bitervo Archuleta. (pg 136b)

2 Oct 1853 – **Jose Romuelo de Jesus Martines**, legit s/ Felipe de Jesus Martines and Maria Antonia Gonsales, residents of el Rito, m. **Maria Ines Aragon**, resident of Rio Arriba, legit d/ Vicente Aragon and Maria Teodora Sisneros; wit/ Julian Alire and Antonio Casados. (pg 136b)

23 Oct 1853 – **Juan de Jesus Trugillo**, legit s/ Jose Ramon Trugillo and Maria Paula Roybal, residents of el Rito, m. **Maria Antonia Vegnina Valdes**, resident of the same place, legit d/ Ramon Valdes and Juana Maria Espinosa; wit/ Julian Alire and Juan Manuel Gallegos. (pg 137)

23 Oct 1853 – **Juan Ysidro Madril**, legit s/ Miguel Madril and Maria Josefa Duran, residents of Tierra Azul, m. **Maria Guadalupe Alire**, resident of el Rito, legit d/ Jose Rafael Alire and Dorotea Trugillo, deceased; wit/ Julian Alire and Juan Manuel Gallegos. (pg 137)

6 Nov 1853 – **Jose de la Cruz Quintana**, legit s/ Miguel Quintana, deceased, and Maria Aguida de Jesus Mestas, residents of el Rito, m. **Maria Venigna de Jesus Sanches**, resident of the same place, legit d/ Alfonso Sanches, deceased, and Geronima Ortis; wit/ Julian Alire and Juan Manuel Gallegos. (pg 137)

17 Nov 1853 – **Jose Maria Chaves**, legit s/ Jose de Jesus Chaves, deceased, and Maria Estefana Lucero, residents of el Rito, m. **Maria Ygnacia Atencio**, resident of the same place, legit d/ Jose Sisilio Atencio and Biviana Quintana; wit/ Julian Alire and Juan Manuel Gallegos. (pg 137b)

17 Nov 1853 – **Jose Felipe Santiago Chacon**, legit s/ Tomas Chacon and Candelaria Ulibarri, residents of el Rito, m. **Getrudis Trugillo**, resident of el Rito, legit d/ Juan Trugillo and Feliciana Quintana; wit/ Julian Alire and Juan Manuel Gallegos. (pg 137b)

20 Nov 1853 – **Jose Vidal Gonsales**, legit s/ Juan Prudencio Gonsales and Maria Juana Vigil, deceased, residents of el Rito, m. **Maria Trinidad Atencio**, resident of el Rito, legit d/ Pablo Atencio and Maria Dolores Martines, deceased; wit/ Julian Alire and Juan Manuel Gallegos. (pg 137b)

28 Nov 1853 – **Jose Guadalupe Varela**, legit s/ Tomas Varela and Maria del Rosario Bruno, residents of Ojo Caliente, m. **Maria Ferminia Valdes**, resident of the same place, legit d/ Juan Ymilio Valdcs and Maria Manucla Martines, deceased; wit/ Jesus Maria Varela and Jose Manuel Martines. (pg 138)

4 Oct 1853 – **Juan Antonio Peña**, legit s/ Rafael Peña and Maria de la Cruz Trugillo, residents of Ojo Caliente, m. **Maria Juliana Sisneros**, resident of the same place, legit d/ Jose Gabriel Sisneros and Maria Albina Maes; wit/ Julian Alire and Juan Manuel Gallegos. (pg 138)

4 Oct 1853 – **Jose Francisco Gallegos**, legit s/ Sandiago Gallegos and Maria de la Lus Lucero, deceased, residents of Ojo Caliente, m. **Maria Concepcion Salas**, resident of the same place, legit d/ Jose Rafael Salas, deceased, and Miguela de Jesus Martines, deceased; wit/ Jesus Maria Varela and Jose Manuel Martines. (pg 138)

4 Oct 1853 – **Andres Corzino Gallegos**, legit s/ Santiago Gallegos and Maria de la Lus Lucero, deceased, residents of Ojo Caliente, m. **Maria Ramona Jaramillo**, resident of the same place, legit d/ Jose Maria Jaramillo, deceased, and Maria Aquirina Abeyta; wit/ Jesus Maria Varela and Jose Manuel Martines. (pg 138b)

8 Oct 1853 – **Gregorio Quintana**, legit s/ Jose Antonio Quintana, deceased, and Ana Maria Lujan, residents of the pueblo of Abiquiu, m. **Maria Dolores Trugillo**, resident of the same place, widow of Juan Vigil, deceased; wit/ Santiago Trugillo and Jose Rafael Duran. (pg 138b)

10 Oct 1853 – **Nerio Montoya**, legit s/ Fernando Montoya and Maria Manuela Sisneros, residents of el Rito, m. **Maria Policarpio Martines**, resident of the same place, legit d/ Felipe Martines and Maria Antonia Garcia; wit/ Julian Alire and Juan Manuel Gallegos. (pg 138b)

16 Oct 1853 – **Jose Vitorio Abran Chaves**, legit s/ Eusebio Antonio Chaves, deceased, and Maria Ysabel Jaques, deceased, resident of Serbiyeta, m. **Maria Soledad Maes**, resident of the same place, legit d/ Santiago Maes and Maria de los Reyes Martines, deceased; wit/ Jesus Maria Varela and Jose Manuel Martines. (pg 139)

This index is inclusive of all names. The groom is noted as (gr) and the bride as (br).

A

Abeyta, Anamaria, 31
Abeyta, Jose Pablo, 42, 44, 45, 49
Abeyta, Jose Ygnacio, 38, 42
Abeyta, Juan (gr), 42
Abeyta, Juan de Jesus, 48
Abeyta, Juan Leonor, 45
Abeyta, Maaria Gertrudis, 38
Abeyta, Maria Acencion (br), 42
Abeyta, Maria Aquirina, 57
Abeyta, Maria Francisca, 42
Abeyta, Maria Gertrudis, 43
Abeyta, Maria Getrudis, 54
Abeyta, Maria Guadalupe (br), 42, 48
Abeyta, Maria Josefa, 38
Abeyta, Maria Luzia (br), 42
Abeyta, Maria Rufina (br), 34
Abeyta, Maria Soledad (br), 38
Abeyta, Miguel Antonio, 34
Abeyta, Pablo, 31, 32, 36, 37, 44, 45, 54, 55
Abeyta, Pablo Antonio, 28, 30, 31, 32, 33,
    34, 35, 36, 37, 38, 41, 42
Abila, Consepcion, 36
Abila, Domingo, 12, 44
Abila, Jose Vicente (gr), 36
Abila, Maria Concepcion, 38
Abila, Maria Dolores, 29
Abila, Maria Josefa, 36
Abila, Maria Tomasa (br), 44
Agilar, Jose Antonio, 18
Agilar, Maria Rafaela (br), 18
Agilar, Paubla, 6
Aguero, Maria de la Merced, 5
Aguilar, Jose Antonio, 20, 39
Aguilar, Maria (br), 34
Aguilar, Maria de Jesus, 40, 42, 44
Aguilar, Maria Soledad (br), 39
Aguilar, Pablo, 34
Ahora, Maria Bibiana de la (br), 40
Ahora, Santiago de la, 40
Alari, Maria Josefa, 13
Alarid, Alaria Josefa, 37

Alarid, Eulogino, 32
Alarid, Gregorio, 34
Alarid, Guadalupe, 13
Alarid, Jose Mariano de Jesus (gr), 5
Alarid, Josefa, 52
Alarid, Juan Andres, 47
Alarid, Juan Jose, 32, 33, 34
Alarid, Juan Jose (gr), 34
Alarid, Juana Maria, 53
Alarid, Manuel, 5
Alarid, Maria del Refugio (br), 47
Alarid, Maria Guadalupe, 5
Alarid, Maria Josefa, 15, 21, 31
Alarid, Maria Manuela (br), 15
Alarid, Miguel, 38
Alire, Jose Manuel, 23, 40, 46
Alire, Jose Rafael, 56
Alire, Jose Rafael (gr), 23
Alire, Juan Antonio, 11
Alire, Juan Antonio (gr), 6
Alire, Juan de Jesus (gr), 54
Alire, Maria Antonia (br), 46
Alire, Maria Gertrudis, 45
Alire, Maria Getrudes, 56
Alire, Maria Guadalupe (br), 56
Alire, Maria Manuela (br), 46
Alire, Maria Pabla (br), 40
Alire, Miguel, 54
Alire, Santiago, 46
Alire, Tomas Antonio, 6
Aliri, Jose Manuel, 15
Apodaca, Juana Maria, 45
Apodaca, Maria Loreta (br), 45
Apodaca, Teodora, 49
Aragon, Antonio Vivian, 38
Aragon, Jose Francisco (gr), 38
Aragon, Maria Dorotea, 47
Aragon, Maria Ines (br), 56
Aragon, Maria Polonia, 35
Aragon, Vicente, 56
Archuleta, Agapita, 31
Archuleta, Antonia Ygnacia, 37
Archuleta, Antonio, 10
Archuleta, Antonio Abad, 36

Archuleta, Antonio Aban, 26
Archuleta, Antonio Casimiro, 33
Archuleta, Antonio Maria (gr), 40
Archuleta, Antonio Rafael (gr), 19
Archuleta, Bitero, 29, 54
Archuleta, Bitoriano (gr), 40
Archuleta, Candelario, 55
Archuleta, Dolores, 8, 10
Archuleta, Francisco, 52, 56
Archuleta, Francisco Antonio, 7
Archuleta, Francisco Antonio (gr), 55
Archuleta, Getrudes, 14
Archuleta, Gregoria, 16
Archuleta, Guadalupe, 12
Archuleta, Jose, 27, 35
Archuleta, Jose Antonio, 51
Archuleta, Jose Antonio (gr), 53
Archuleta, Jose Manuel de Jesus (gr), 52
Archuleta, Jose Miguel, 2, 30, 44, 54
Archuleta, Jose Miguel de, 40
Archuleta, Jose Pablo, 18, 19
Archuleta, Jose Ramon, 40
Archuleta, Jose Tomas de Aquino (gr), 45
Archuleta, Juan Andres, 18
Archuleta, Juan Antonio, 18
Archuleta, Juan Balentin (gr), 33
Archuleta, Juan Francisco (gr), 10
Archuleta, Juan Nepomuceno (gr), 54
Archuleta, Juana Maria, 36
Archuleta, Juana Maria (br), 26, 35
Archuleta, Luciano, 41
Archuleta, Lusiano, 29
Archuleta, Manuel, 53, 54
Archuleta, Manuel de Jesus, 23
Archuleta, Manuel de Jesus (gr), 56
Archuleta, Marcial, 15
Archuleta, Maria Antonia (br), 37
Archuleta, Maria Catalina (br), 44
Archuleta, Maria Conscepcion, 13
Archuleta, Maria de la Lus, 12, 22
Archuleta, Maria de la Lus (br), 9
Archuleta, Maria Dolores, 17, 29
Archuleta, Maria Dolores (br), 23
Archuleta, Maria Elena (br), 10
Archuleta, Maria Feliciana (br), 23
Archuleta, Maria Francisca (br), 35

Archuleta, Maria Gertrudiz, 43
Archuleta, Maria Getrudes, 13, 14
Archuleta, Maria Getrudis, 29
Archuleta, Maria Jetrudes, 16, 31
Archuleta, Maria Juana, 15, 50
Archuleta, Maria Juana (br), 15
Archuleta, Maria Juana Guadalupe (br), 10
Archuleta, Maria Luisa, 40
Archuleta, Maria Manuela, 33, 42
Archuleta, Maria Matiana (br), 54
Archuleta, Maria Paubla (br), 39
Archuleta, Maria Rita, 13
Archuleta, Maria Romualda (br), 27
Archuleta, Maria Rosalia (br), 51
Archuleta, Maria Vicenta, 34, 35
Archuleta, Maria Ygnes (br), 29
Archuleta, Miguel, 35, 37
Archuleta, Nestor, 29
Archuleta, Nicolas, 10, 23, 45
Archuleta, Nicolas (gr), 30
Archuleta, Pantalion (gr), 18
Archuleta, Pasqual Bailon (gr), 13
Archuleta, Thomas de Aquino (gr), 18
Archuleta, Tomas (gr), 53
Archuleta, Vicente (gr), 36
Archuleta, Ygnacio, 29, 38, 42
Armijo, Maria Nicolasa, 8, 13
Armijo, Maria Ruperta, 45
Atencio, Eilario, 16
Atencio, Francisco (gr), 44
Atencio, Francisco Antonio, 37, 46
Atencio, Gregorio de Jesus (gr), 7
Atencio, Jose Agapito (gr), 37
Atencio, Jose Cisilio (gr), 14
Atencio, Jose Justo (gr), 20
Atencio, Jose Manuel, 9, 15, 20
Atencio, Jose Maria, 36
Atencio, Jose Pablo (gr), 15
Atencio, Jose Ramon (gr), 9
Atencio, Jose Sisilio, 57
Atencio, Juan, 11, 14, 22
Atencio, Juan Francisco, 15
Atencio, Juan Francisco (gr), 17
Atencio, Juan Manuel, 20
Atencio, Juan Ygnacio, 7

Atencio, Juana Maria (br), 44
Atencio, Julian, 14, 22
Atencio, Manuel, 13, 17
Atencio, Maria Cecilia (br), 7
Atencio, Maria de la Cruz (br), 16
Atencio, Maria de la Lus, 6
Atencio, Maria de la Lus (br), 42
Atencio, Maria Josefa, 7
Atencio, Maria Juliana (br), 46
Atencio, Maria Manuela (br), 20
Atencio, Maria Paula, 25
Atencio, Maria Rosa (br), 39
Atencio, Maria Rosalia, 56
Atencio, Maria Trinidad (br), 57
Atencio, Maria Ygnacia (br), 57
Atencio, Miguel, 1, 11, 17
Atencio, Miguel (gr), 22
Atencio, Miguel Asencio, 7
Atencio, Pablo, 57
Atencio, Paubla, 53
Atencio, Pedro, 11, 40, 42, 44
Atencio, Pedro Antonio, 20
Atencio, Romualda, 22
Atencio, Rosalia, 9
Atencio, Ygnacio (gr), 11
Atencio, Ylario, 44
Atencio, Ylario (gr), 40
Atensio, Jose Manuel, 30

B

Baca, Anna Maria Clara, 42
Baca, Baltasar, 12
Baca, Baltasar (gr), 5
Baca, Barbara, 51
Baca, Francisco Tomas (gr), 33
Baca, Guadalupe, 6, 10, 17
Baca, Jose Albino (gr), 51
Baca, Jose Manuel (gr), 38
Baca, Jose Pedro Benavides Maria, 30
Baca, Juan Nepomuseno, 10
Baca, Maria Antonia, 17
Baca, Maria Clara, 49, 51
Baca, Maria de Jesus (br), 42
Baca, Maria Guadalupe, 16
Baca, Maria Juliana, 49

Baca, Maria Manuela, 18
Baca, Maria Rita, 44, 49
Baca, Maria Sabina, 38
Baca, Maria Soledad, 39
Baca, Nepomuceno, 6
Baca, Pablo, 43
Baca, Paula, 5
Baca, Rafael, 4, 5, 9, 10, 12, 14, 17, 21, 38
Balasques, Maria Concepcion, 38
Balasques, Maria de la Luz, 3
Balberde, Maria de Jesus, 8
Balberde, Vibiana, 9
Baldes, Anamaria (br), 31
Baldes, Anna Maria, 36
Baldes, Antonio de la Cruz (gr), 3
Baldes, Antonio Jose, 2, 31
Baldes, Bernardo, 4, 18
Baldes, Crus, 16
Baldes, Cruz, 13, 16
Baldes, Diego, 3
Baldes, Diego Antonio (gr), 10
Baldes, Eusebio, 10
Baldes, Feliciana, 6
Baldes, Francisco, 8
Baldes, German, 2, 7
Baldes, Grabriel, 14
Baldes, Guadalupe, 13, 16
Baldes, Jose de la Cruz, 3
Baldes, Jose Eusebio, 3
Baldes, Jose Francisco, 2
Baldes, Jose Francisco (gr), 2, 12
Baldes, Jose Gabriel (gr), 18
Baldes, Jose Manuel, 2, 13
Baldes, Jose Miguel, 9, 10
Baldes, Jose Rafael, 2
Baldes, Juan, 15
Baldes, Juan Jose, 12
Baldes, Juan Pio (gr), 2
Baldes, Juana Catarina, 14
Baldes, Julian, 16
Baldes, Manuel, 4, 14
Baldes, Manuel Lorenzo (gr), 6
Baldes, Manuela, 11
Baldes, Maria Antonia (br), 2, 14
Baldes, Maria Barbara (br), 4
Baldes, Maria de Jesus, 4

Baldes, Maria de la Cruz, 6
Baldes, Maria de la Cruz (br), 13
Baldes, Maria de las Nieves (br), 10
Baldes, Maria de los Reyes, 5, 7, 10
Baldes, Maria de los Reyes (br), 7
Baldes, Maria Inez, 2
Baldes, Maria Manuela, 3
Baldes, Maria Manuela (br), 6
Baldes, Maria Miquela (br), 17
Baldes, Maria Paubla (br), 16
Baldes, Maria Rafaela, 4
Baldes, Maria Rita (br), 6, 7
Baldes, Maria Rufina (br), 17
Baldes, Maria Soledad, 6
Baldes, Maria Viviana, 4
Baldes, Maria Ygnacia, 7
Baldes, Maria Ygnacia (br), 15
Baldes, Mariano, 6, 30, 31
Baldes, Miguel, 9
Baldes, Nicolas, 6
Baldes, Pedro Antonio (gr), 9
Baldes, Rafael, 2, 6, 17
Baldes, Santiago, 6
Baldes, Santiago (gr), 16
Baldes, Thomas, 16
Baldes, Tomas, 17
Baldes, Trenidad, 3
Baldes, Ygnacio, 4
Baldez, Maria Manuela, 43
Ballejos, Jose Maria, 40
Balverde, Maria de la Lus, 26
Barela, Antonia, 22
Barela, Cristobal, 27
Barela, Diego, 12
Barela, Diego Antonio, 34
Barela, Maria Josefa (br), 27
Barela, Maria Soledad (br), 12
Barela, Mariano (gr), 34
Bargas, Maria Rita, 46
Baros, Maria Antonia, 26, 32
Basques, Agustin, 44
Basques, Juan Agustin (gr), 44
Beita, Jose Pablo, 14
Beita, Jose Pablo (gr), 13
Beita, Josefa, 6
Beita, Juan, 18

Beita, Juan Nepomuceno, 24
Beita, Maria Dolores (br), 24
Beita, Maria Guadalupe, 5
Beita, Maria Josefa, 14, 24
Beita, Miguel Antonio, 6
Beita, Pablo, 13
Beitia, Maria Gertrudes, 26
Belarde, Encarnacion, 5
Belarde, Maria Margarita, 16
Belarde, Rosalia, 1, 5
Belasques, Antonio Jose (gr), 36
Belasques, Jose Antonio, 37
Belasques, Jose Gabriel (gr), 36
Belasques, Jose Joaquin, 48
Belasques, Josefa, 8
Belasques, Juan Antonio, 12
Belasques, Juana Maria, 7
Belasques, Juaquin, 36
Belasques, Maria de la Lus, 50
Belasques, Maria Juana, 6
Belasques, Maria Natividad (br), 52
Belasques, Maria Trinidad (br), 47
Belasques, Pedro Ygnacio (gr), 12
Belasques, Ygnacio, 52
Belasques. Quirino (gr), 48
Benabides, Dolores, 14
Benabides, Estevan, 14
Benabides, Jose Antonio, 17
Benabides, Maria Dolores, 51
Benabides, Maria Dolores (br), 17, 24
Benavedes, Maria Ygnacia, 1
Benavides, Pedro, 30
Bernal, Maria Petra, 10
Bernal, Petra, 12
Bernal. Polonia, 17
Blea, Maria de la Lus, 16
Bruno, Maria del Rosario, 57
Bustos, Maria Rita, 25
Butierres, Maria Candelaria (br), 42
Butierres, Miguel Antonio, 42

C

Cabesa de Baca, Maria Gertrudis, 51
Casado, Maria Isabel, 30
Casados, Jose Ygnacio, 9

Casados, Maria Isabel, 44
Casados, Maria Serafina (br), 9
Casados, Maria Ysabel, 40
Casias, Antonio (gr), 34
Casias, Felipe, 34, 40, 46
Casias, Jose, 41
Casias, Jose de la Encarnacion, 43
Casias, Jose Encarnacion, 34
Casias, Jose Polinario (gr), 43
Casias, Manuela, 6
Casias, Maria Juana (br), 41
Casillas, Maria del Carmel, 36
Castelo, Juan Nepomuseno (gr), 36
Castelo, Maria Juana (br), 24
Castelo, Maria Manuela, 24
Castelo, Mariano, 24, 36
Castillo, Josefa del, 33
Castillo, Juan Jose, 22
Castillo, Juan Jose (gr), 22
Castillo, Maria Dolores, 52
Castillo, Maria Victoria del, 47
Chabes, Agustin, 9, 10, 19, 20, 21, 23
Chabes, Jose Antonio (gr), 23
Chabes, Juan, 9
Chabes, Juan Agustin, 23
Chabes, Juan Christobal, 9
Chabes, Juan Miguel, 21
Chabes, Maria de Jesus, 21
Chabes, Maria de Jesus (br), 21
Chabes, Maria de la Luz (br), 22
Chabes, Maria Ygnacia, 19
Chabez, Antonio Jose, 22
Chacon, Albina, 38
Chacon, Amado Ygnacio, 26
Chacon, Getrudis, 53
Chacon, Jose Felipe Santiago (gr), 57
Chacon, Jose Maria (gr), 8
Chacon, Jose Miguel (gr), 23
Chacon, Jose Tomas (gr), 23
Chacon, Juan de Jesus, 31
Chacon, Juan Faustin (gr), 18
Chacon, Juan Gabriel, 50
Chacon, Juan Gabriel (gr), 26
Chacon, Maria de la Luz, 1
Chacon, Maria Dolores, 33, 50
Chacon, Maria Dolores (br), 18

Chacon, Maria Gertrudes (br), 18
Chacon, Maria Guadalupe (br), 31
Chacon, Maria Manuela, 17, 30
Chacon, Maria Nestora (br), 29
Chacon, Maria Sipriana (br), 16
Chacon, Noberto, 23, 47
Chacon, Thomas, 10
Chacon, Tomas, 9, 57
Chacon, Tomas de Jesus, 3, 7
Chacon, Ygnacio, 8, 16, 18
Chaves, Ana Maria, 29, 50
Chaves, Antonio, 2
Chaves, Domingo, 2
Chaves, Eusebio, 38
Chaves, Eusebio Antonio, 58
Chaves, Francisco Antonio, 1, 5
Chaves, Francisco Esteban, 29, 36, 37, 38, 39, 40, 41, 42, 43, 48
Chaves, Jose, 1, 12, 17
Chaves, Jose Antonio, 28
Chaves, Jose de Jesus, 2, 57
Chaves, Jose Manuel, 30
Chaves, Jose Maria, 29
Chaves, Jose Maria (gr), 1, 57
Chaves, Jose Maria del Socorro, 2
Chaves, Jose Patricio, 31
Chaves, Jose Sabino (gr), 2
Chaves, Jose Vitorio Abran (gr), 58
Chaves, Juan Agustin, 3, 5, 12, 16, 28, 29, 30, 31, 37, 38, 39, 40, 41, 42, 43, 44, 47, 48, 49, 52
Chaves, Juan Andres (gr), 47
Chaves, Juan Antonio, 40
Chaves, Juan Antonio (gr), 9
Chaves, Juan Bernardo, 22
Chaves, Juan Jose, 17
Chaves, Juana Maria, 33
Chaves, Julian, 49
Chaves, Manuela, 16
Chaves, Marcos, 49
Chaves, Maria Andrea de los, 28
Chaves, Maria Ascencion (br), 22
Chaves, Maria Clara (br), 38
Chaves, Maria de la Lus, 40, 55
Chaves, Maria de la Lus (br), 12, 49
Chaves, Maria de la Luz, 5

Chaves, Maria del Rosario (br), 55
Chaves, Maria Dolores, 3, 20
Chaves, Maria Encarnacion, 31
Chaves, Maria Joaquina, 2
Chaves, Maria Josefa, 32
Chaves, Maria Josefa (br), 1, 45
Chaves, Maria Juana, 2
Chaves, Maria Manuela, 43, 48
Chaves, Maria Micaela, 3, 49
Chaves, Maria Miguela, 56
Chaves, Maria Paula, 46
Chaves, Maria Relles, 30
Chaves, Maria Teodora Salome, 2
Chaves, Maria Ygnacia, 2, 12, 30
Chaves, Maria Ysidora (br), 40, 48
Chaves, Mariano Antonio (gr), 5
Chaves, Matias (gr), 17
Chaves, Miguel, 5
Chaves, Rael, 11
Chaves, Tomas (gr), 2, 7
Chaves, Vicente (gr), 49
Chavez, Antonio, 30
Chavez, Jose Maria, 44
Chavez, Maria Gregoria (br), 30
Chavez, Maria Manuela (br), 44
Coca, Maria de las Niebes, 48
Copa, Juan Manuel, 27
Cordoba, Bitor, 55
Cordoba, Juan de Jesus, 22
Cordoba, Juan Manuel, 43
Cordoba, Maria Simona (br), 22
Cordoba, Ramon, 11, 40, 47
Cordova, Felipe (gr), 4
Cordova, Jose Ramon (gr), 6
Cordova, Manuel, 4
Cordova, Ramon, 32
Coris, Maria Manuela, 23, 52
Cortes, Jose, 55
Cortes, Jose (gr), 55
Crispin, Jose Miguel, 30
Crispin, Juana Maria (br), 30

D

Deaguero, Juan Jose (gr), 36
Delgado, Estefana, 40

Delgado, Jose Manuel, 6
Delgado, Jose Manuel (gr), 16
Delgado, Marcos, 13, 16, 18
Delgado, Maria de Jesus, 13, 51
Delgado, Maria de Jesus (br), 13
Delgado, Maria Josefa, 6
Derrera, Maria Manuela, 30
Domingues, Antonio Jose (gr), 45
Domingues, Jose, 45
Duran, Antonio Aban (gr), 4
Duran, Antonio de Jesus (gr), 42
Duran, Crecencio, 48
Duran, Diego, 48
Duran, Joaquina, 1
Duran, Jose, 33
Duran, Jose Andres (gr), 48
Duran, Jose Dolores (gr), 55
Duran, Jose Fernando, 42
Duran, Jose Rafael, 1, 8, 15, 16, 17, 18, 19,
    21, 25, 52, 57
Duran, Juan de Jesus (gr), 55
Duran, Juan Jose (gr), 6
Duran, Juana, 49
Duran, Maria Brigida, 44
Duran, Maria Concepcion, 21
Duran, Maria de Refugio (br), 34
Duran, Maria Dolores, 39
Duran, Maria Gertrudis, 47
Duran, Maria Josefa, 28, 45, 56
Duran, Maria Patrocinia (br), 6
Duran, Maria Paula, 23
Duran, Maria Paula (br), 33
Duran, Pablo, 4, 50
Duran, Paula, 20
Duran, Visente, 6
Duran, Yisdro, 55

E

Errera, Felipe de, 25
Errera, Felipe de Jesus de (gr), 24
Errera, Francisca de, 13
Errera, Maria Manuela de, 20
Errera, Maria Ramona (br), 25
Errera, Maria Ygnacia de (br), 25
Espinosa, Ana Maria, 20

Espinosa, Antonio, 2, 8, 14, 16, 31, 43
Espinosa, Asencio, 3
Espinosa, Diego Antonio (gr), 7
Espinosa, Donaciano (gr), 43
Espinosa, Felipe Santiago (gr), 8
Espinosa, Francisco, 7, 43, 51
Espinosa, Francisco Antonio (gr), 31
Espinosa, Jose Alejandro, 41
Espinosa, Jose Aniceto (gr), 41
Espinosa, Jose Antonio, 22
Espinosa, Jose Antonio Alejandro (gr), 17
Espinosa, Jose Gabriel (gr), 22
Espinosa, Josefa, 14, 17, 21
Espinosa, Juan Antonio, 31
Espinosa, Juan Bautista, 41
Espinosa, Juan de la Cruz (gr), 51
Espinosa, Juan Jose, 52
Espinosa, Juan Jose (gr), 20
Espinosa, Juan Pedro, 20
Espinosa, Juana Maria, 56
Espinosa, Julian, 45
Espinosa, Maria Antonia, 9
Espinosa, Maria Barbara, 19, 25
Espinosa, Maria Candelaria, 54
Espinosa, Maria Josefa, 31
Espinosa, Maria Lorensa, 12
Espinosa, Maria Lugarada, 15
Espinosa, Maria Lugarda, 2, 19, 30, 45
Espinosa, Maria Pabla (br), 37
Espinosa, Maria Ramona, 30
Espinosa, Maria Rosa, 22
Espinosa, Maria Rufina, 46
Espinosa, Maria Ruperta (br), 45
Espinosa, Nicolas, 10
Espinosa, Pedro, 37, 50
Espinosa, Ramon, 37
Espinosa, Ramon Antonio (gr), 10
Espinoza, Maria Manuela, 52

F

Fageda, Josefa, 39
Fernandes, Maria de la Luz, 33, 42
Flores, Maria Paubla, 16
Forangas, Maria Soledad, 50
Fresquis, Rafael, 50

G

Galbes, Felipe, 4
Galbes, Jose Guadalupe (gr), 4
Galbes, Jose Juan, 4
Galbis, Felipe, 6
Galbis, Juan, 28
Galbis, Maria del Carmen, 49
Galbis, Maria Feliciana (br), 28
Galbis, Maria Rosalia (br), 6
Gallego, Barbara Antonia, 9
Gallego, Diego, 25
Gallego, Domingo, 7, 19, 25
Gallego, Felipe Santiago, 5
Gallego, Jose, 5, 12, 25
Gallego, Jose Pablo, 5, 17
Gallego, Jose Ygnacio, 4
Gallego, Juan Antonio (gr), 19, 25
Gallego, Juan Bautista (gr), 21
Gallego, Juan de Jesus, 9
Gallego, Juan de Jesus (gr), 5
Gallego, Juan Manuel, 53
Gallego, Juana Nepomuceno, 15
Gallego, Juana Nepomusena (br), 11
Gallego, Julian, 26, 27
Gallego, Manuel, 11, 23, 28
Gallego, Manuel Antonio (gr), 25
Gallego, Manuel Gregorio (gr), 25
Gallego, Maria Agreda (br), 25
Gallego, Maria Asencion, 17
Gallego, Maria Concepcion (br), 26
Gallego, Maria de la Atencio, 5
Gallego, Maria de la Cruz, 4
Gallego, Maria del Carmen, 15, 23
Gallego, Maria Fabriana (br), 17
Gallego, Maria Francisca (br), 12
Gallego, Maria Gertrudes, 22
Gallego, Maria Gertrudes (br), 27
Gallego, Maria Luisa, 9
Gallego, Maria Luiza, 27
Gallego, Maria Manuela, 21, 26
Gallego, Maria Nicolasa, 9
Gallego, Maria Rosalia (br), 7
Gallego, Maria Teodora (br), 4, 5
Gallego, Maria Theodora, 4
Gallego, Miguel Acencio, 21

Gallego, Miguel Antonio, 1, 4, 22
Gallego, Miguel Antonio (gr), 28
Gallego, Miguel Ascencio, 17
Gallego, Pedro, 12
Gallego, Rafael, 25, 26
Gallego, Ygnacia, 18
Gallegos, Andres Corzino (gr), 57
Gallegos, Antonia Maria, 33
Gallegos, Antonio, 41
Gallegos, Antonio Ysabel, 35
Gallegos, Bacilio (gr), 41
Gallegos, Bernabel (gr), 51
Gallegos, Dolores, 54
Gallegos, Domingo, 38, 40, 41, 53
Gallegos, Eniceta, 41
Gallegos, Eulogio, 38, 54
Gallegos, Felipe, 33, 34, 35, 36, 40, 41, 42, 43
Gallegos, Francisca, 49
Gallegos, Geronimo, 34, 35, 47, 49, 51, 52
Gallegos, Guadalupe, 36, 37, 48
Gallegos, Guadalupe (gr), 49
Gallegos, Jose de la Lus, 41, 43, 51
Gallegos, Jose de los Relles (gr), 39
Gallegos, Jose Francisco (gr), 57
Gallegos, Jose Gabriel (gr), 50
Gallegos, Jose Manuel, 47
Gallegos, Jose Miguel, 53
Gallegos, Jose Miguel (gr), 35
Gallegos, Juan Antonio, 47
Gallegos, Juan Jose, 50
Gallegos, Juan Jose (gr), 30, 44
Gallegos, Juan Manuel, 53, 54, 56, 57
Gallegos, Juan Ysidro (gr), 53
Gallegos, Julian (gr), 32
Gallegos, Manuel, 32, 50, 51
Gallegos, Maria Aniceta, 36
Gallegos, Maria Barbara, 28, 51
Gallegos, Maria Bentura, 35
Gallegos, Maria Bernarda (br), 40
Gallegos, Maria Carmelia, 51
Gallegos, Maria Consepcion, 7
Gallegos, Maria Dolores (br), 51
Gallegos, Maria Feliciana, 30
Gallegos, Maria Gertrudis, 42
Gallegos, Maria Getrudis, 6

Gallegos, Maria Guadalupe (br), 32
Gallegos, Maria Josefa (br), 53, 54
Gallegos, Maria Loreta, 41, 43
Gallegos, Maria Luisa, 2
Gallegos, Maria Madalena, 31
Gallegos, Maria Marselina, 35
Gallegos, Maria Nepomusena, 43
Gallegos, Maria Petrona (br), 40
Gallegos, Maria Rafaela, 48
Gallegos, Maria Rita (br), 51
Gallegos, Maria Ruperta (br), 33
Gallegos, Maria Sipriana (br), 54
Gallegos, Maria Ypolita, 31
Gallegos, Mariano (gr), 52
Gallegos, Miguel, 46, 54
Gallegos, Miguel Antonio, 51
Gallegos, Rafael, 37, 39, 40, 41, 42, 43, 44
Gallegos, Rafael (gr), 38
Gallegos, Rafael Antonio, 30
Gallegos, Roman, 52
Gallegos, Rosalia, 36
Gallegos, Sandiago, 57
Gallegos, Santiago, 40, 50, 57
Gallegos, Yniceta, 39
Galles, Migel Antonio, 31
Galvis, Jose Felis, 30
Galvis, Jose Leonides (gr), 39
Galvis, Juan Jose, 39
Garcia de la Mora, Jose Santiago, 10
Garcia de la Mora, Jose Santiago (gr), 8
Garcia de la Mora. Atencio de Jesus, 8
Garcia,
    Maria Natividad, 46
    Maria Natividad (br), 53
Garcia, Antonio, 21, 22, 25, 34
Garcia, Antonio Jose, 14, 28, 33
Garcia, Antonio Maria (gr), 41
Garcia, Bernardo (gr), 52
Garcia, Concepcion, 42
Garcia, Dolores, 6
Garcia, Encarnacion, 52
Garcia, Felipe, 15, 22
Garcia, Felipe Santiago, 3, 19
Garcia, Francisco Estevan (gr), 12
Garcia, Guadalupe, 41, 50
Garcia, Jesus Maria, 26

Garcia, Jesus Maria (gr), 25, 41
Garcia, Jose Antonio, 25
Garcia, Jose Antonio (gr), 54
Garcia, Jose Candelario, 13
Garcia, Jose Cristobal (gr), 19
Garcia, Jose de Jesus (gr), 14
Garcia, Jose Maria, 8, 23, 52
Garcia, Jose Pablo, 38, 43, 54
Garcia, Jose Rafael (gr), 33
Garcia, Jose Ramon (gr), 19
Garcia, Jose Ramon Blas (gr), 19
Garcia, Jose Tomas (gr), 35
Garcia, Josefa, 6, 55
Garcia, Juan Antonio, 19, 41
Garcia, Juan de Jesus, 3
Garcia, Juan de Jesus (gr), 1
Garcia, Juan de los Reyes (gr), 34
Garcia, Juan Esteban, 12
Garcia, Juan Luis, 19
Garcia, Juana Maria, 22
Garcia, Juana Rosalia (br), 23
Garcia, Lorenso, 28
Garcia, Manuel, 1, 19
Garcia, Manuel (gr), 43
Garcia, Manuel Visente, 10
Garcia, Manuela, 11
Garcia, Maria, 50
Garcia, Maria Alta Gracia, 31
Garcia, Maria Andrea, 32
Garcia, Maria Andrea (br), 13, 22
Garcia, Maria Andres, 31
Garcia, Maria Antonia, 7, 15, 34, 57
Garcia, Maria Biviana (br), 26
Garcia, Maria Candelaria, 23
Garcia, Maria Concepcion (br), 55
Garcia, Maria Consepcion, 52
Garcia, Maria Conspecion (br), 9
Garcia, Maria de Jesus, 3
Garcia, Maria de la Luz, 28
Garcia, Maria de los Luz, 47
Garcia, Maria de Marta, 30
Garcia, Maria Dolores, 16, 35, 49
Garcia, Maria Dorotea, 4
Garcia, Maria Francisca, 32
Garcia, Maria Josefa, 4
Garcia, Maria Josefa (br), 19, 41

Garcia, Maria Juana (br), 38
Garcia, Maria Luisa (br), 28
Garcia, Maria Manuela, 5, 20
Garcia, Maria Manuela (br), 28
Garcia, Maria Rita (br), 20
Garcia, Maria Rosalia (br), 11
Garcia, Maria Salaome, 42
Garcia, Maria Trinidad, 53
Garcia, Maria Trinidad (br), 53
Garcia, Mariano, 55
Garcia, Mariano (gr), 22
Garcia, Martina, 20
Garcia, Miguel, 1, 27, 35
Garcia, Nicolas, 18
Garcia, Nicolasa, 53
Garcia, Pablo, 26, 49
Garcia, Pedro Antonio (gr), 50
Garcia, Rafael, 14
Garcia, Salbador, 41
Garcia, Salbador Manuel (gr), 10
Garcia, Sieto, 20
Garcia, Sisto, 9, 12
Garcia, Ysidora, 47
Garduño, Maria Teodora, 28
Gillen, Jose Manuel, 12, 13
Gillen, Juan Ysidro, 10
Gillen, Maria Francisca, 13
Gillen, Maria Ramona, 10
Gillen, Maria Ramona (br), 12
Giron, Maria Polonia, 46, 55
Gomes, Antonio Nerio (gr), 12
Gomes, Felipe, 10, 12
Gomes, Fileto, 36
Gomes, Gaspar, 18
Gomes, Jose Pedro, 22, 30, 52
Gomes, Josefa, 27, 51
Gomes, Juan, 10
Gomes, Juan Andres (gr), 37
Gomes, Juan de Jesus (gr), 18
Gomes, Maria del Carmen (br), 22
Gomes, Maria Dolores, 10
Gomes, Maria Francisca (br), 9
Gomes, Maria Guadalupe (br), 36
Gomes, Maria Josefa, 2, 7, 33
Gomes, Maria Josefa (br), 24
Gomes, Maria Juana (br), 17

Gomes, Maria Manuela, 31
Gomes, Maria Pabla, 38
Gomes, Maria Paula, 44
Gomes, Maria Paula (br), 30
Gomes, Maria Ruperta (br), 52
Gomes, Maria Soledad, 24
Gomes, Mariano Mateo, 17
Gomes, Pedro, 11, 36, 37, 50
Gomes. Juana Maria (br), 10
Gonsales, Estefana, 48
Gonsales, Francisco, 28
Gonsales, Francisco (gr), 53
Gonsales, Jose Antonio, 26
Gonsales, Jose de la Crus (gr), 20
Gonsales, Jose Dolores (gr), 26
Gonsales, Jose Francisco (gr), 47
Gonsales, Jose Maria, 49
Gonsales, Jose Vicente (gr), 11
Gonsales, Jose Vidal (gr), 57
Gonsales, Juan Cristobal, 23
Gonsales, Juan de Jesus (gr), 7
Gonsales, Juan Felipe, 15, 16
Gonsales, Juan Prudencio, 57
Gonsales, Juan Prudencio (gr), 15, 26
Gonsales, Juana Catarina, 51
Gonsales, Juana Maria (br), 14
Gonsales, Manuela, 52
Gonsales, Maria Antonia, 56
Gonsales, Maria Bibiana (br), 25
Gonsales, Maria de la Cruz, 15
Gonsales, Maria de la Lus (br), 32
Gonsales, Maria Felisiana (br), 49
Gonsales, Maria Guadalupe (br), 28
Gonsales, Maria Manuela, 52
Gonsales, Maria Manuela (br), 23
Gonsales, Maria Teodora, 18
Gonsales, Maria Tomasa (br), 25
Gonsales, Pablo, 25, 53
Gonsales, Pascual, 32
Gonsales, Pasqual, 14, 18
Gonsales, Salbador, 9, 18, 47
Gonzales, Jose, 5
Gonzales, Juan Antonio, 1, 5
Gonzales, Maria Juana (br), 5
Gonzales, Maria Luisa (br), 5
Gonzales, Vicente, 16

Griego, Juan de Jesus, 1
Griego, Maria Manuela (br), 1
Griego, Maria Martina, 36
Griego, Maria Soledad, 1
Guillen, Jose Manuel, 21
Guillen, Maria Casilda (br), 3
Guillen, Maria Luisa (br), 21
Guillen, Maria Ramona, 55
Gurule, Jose Teodoro (gr), 49
Gurule, Juan, 42, 49, 51
Gurule, Juan Antonio, 3
Gurule, Juan Antonio (gr), 10
Gurule, Maria Rosalia (br), 3
Gutierres, Antonio, 1, 6, 8, 14, 15, 20, 32
Gutierres, Joaquin (gr), 5
Gutierres, Jose Antonio, 49
Gutierres, Jose Manuel (gr), 32
Gutierres, Juan, 1, 2, 3, 5, 10, 16, 21, 23, 24, 25
Gutierres, Juan Francisco, 17
Gutierres, Juaquin, 51
Gutierres, Manuel (gr), 17
Gutierres, Maria Antonia, 5
Gutierres, Maria Dolores, 12
Gutierres, Maria Encarnacion (br), 5
Gutierres, Maria Estefana (br), 23
Gutierres, Maria Francisca (br), 49
Gutierres, Maria Gracia (br), 51
Gutierres, Maria Manuela, 15
Gutierres, Pasqual, 5
Gutierrez, Juan, 18
Gutierrez, Maria Manuela, 21

H

Herrera, Cristobal de, 34
Herrera, Crus, 17
Herrera, Felipe de, 25
Herrera, Jesus Maria de (gr), 43
Herrera, Jose, 27
Herrera, Jose Antonio, 1
Herrera, Jose Miguel de, 46
Herrera, Jose Vicente de (gr), 34
Herrera, Juan de Jesus (gr), 17, 27
Herrera, Juan de Jesus de, 56
Herrera, Juan de la Cruz de, 43

Herrera, Juan Pedro de (gr), 1
Herrera, Manuel Gregorio de (gr), 43
Herrera, Manuela, 9
Herrera, Maria Aniceta de (br), 36
Herrera, Maria Concepcion, 39
Herrera, Maria Consecpcion de, 4
Herrera, Maria Estefana de (br), 56
Herrera, Maria Soledad de, 55
Herrera, Pedro Antonio de, 36
Herrera, Pedro Antonio de (gr), 46, 54
Herrera, Pedro de, 48
Herrera, Rumalda de, 35
Herrera, Seledon, 17

J

Jacques, Felipe, 27
Jacques, Maria Guadalupe (br), 27
Jacques, Maria Pacifica, 16
Jageva, Maria Josefa, 35
Jaques, Felipe, 3, 18, 49, 56
Jaques, Juan Bautista (gr), 56
Jaques, Juan de Jesus, 45
Jaques, Juan Manuel, 4
Jaques, Maria Agustina (br), 49
Jaques, Maria Gertrudis, 9, 37, 44
Jaques, Maria Getrudis, 8
Jaques, Maria Josefa (br), 17
Jaques, Maria Manuela (br), 3
Jaques, Maria Pacifica, 18, 22
Jaques, Maria Soledad (br), 4
Jaques, Maria Ysabel, 58
Jaques, Pasifica, 17
Jaques, Rafael (gr), 45
Jaques, Ysabel, 11, 38
Jaramiilo, Maria Manuela, 19
Jaramillo, Ana Maria, 14, 18, 21
Jaramillo, Ana Maria (br), 5
Jaramillo, Anamaria, 16
Jaramillo, Anna Maria, 30
Jaramillo, Antonio Maria (gr), 32
Jaramillo, Antonio Romaldo (gr), 22
Jaramillo, Diego Antonio, 44, 55
Jaramillo, Dolores, 31
Jaramillo, Eugenio (gr), 50
Jaramillo, Francisco Antonio, 29

Jaramillo, Geronimo, 36, 39, 41, 47, 50
Jaramillo, Gregorio, 8
Jaramillo, Jose Antonio, 2, 25
Jaramillo, Jose Bicente, 40
Jaramillo, Jose Maria, 57
Jaramillo, Jose Miguel, 7, 17, 19, 50
Jaramillo, Juan Agustin, 5, 7, 24, 35
Jaramillo, Juan Jose (gr), 6
Jaramillo, Juan Manuel, 6, 22
Jaramillo, Maria Acencion, 50
Jaramillo, Maria Antonia, 32
Jaramillo, Maria Andrea (br), 2
Jaramillo, Maria Asencion (br), 44
Jaramillo, Maria de Jesus Esquipula (br), 50
Jaramillo, Maria de la Lus (br), 24
Jaramillo, Maria del Refugio (br), 19
Jaramillo, Maria Guadalupe (br), 11, 22
Jaramillo, Maria Josefa (br), 55
Jaramillo, Maria Manuela, 15, 48
Jaramillo, Maria Pamuela, 7
Jaramillo, Maria Ramona (br), 57
Jaramillo, Maria Salome (br), 35
Jaramillo, Natividad (br), 52
Jaramillo, Patricio, 19, 22, 32
Jaramillo, Pedro, 50
Jaramillo, Pedro Antonio (gr), 25
Jaramillo, Rafaela, 2, 11
Jaramillo, Ramon, 52
Jaramiyo, Maria Gertrudes, 10
Jaramiyo, Pedro, 10, 14
Jarmillo, Jose Manuel, 17
Jiron, Jose Damian, 28
Jiron, Jose Maria (gr), 49
Jiron, Juan Emilio, 49
Jiron, Maria del Carmel, 33
Jiron, Maria del Carmen, 24
Jiron, Maria Pascuala, 34, 50
Jiron, Maria Polonia, 45

L

Lao, Jose de, 11
Lao, Santiago de (gr), 11
Lara, Maria Ygnacia, 50
Leal, Maria Moncerrate, 10

Leal, Maria Monserrate de, 33
Lente, Juan (gr), 48
Lente, Manuel, 48
Lobato, Antonio, 50
Lobato, Baltasar, 46
Lobato, Candelario (gr), 50
Lobato, Jose Deciderio (gr), 46
Lobato, Maria Antonia (br), 31
Lobato, Maria de los Reyes, 9, 12, 20
Lobato, Maria de los Reyes (br), 39
Lobato, Maria Leonisia, 47
Lobato, Maria Lionisia, 38
Lobato, Maria Manuela, 40
Lobato, Migel Antonio, 31
Lobato, Pedro Antonio, 39
Lobato, Reyes, 19
Lobato, Roberta, 47
Lopes, Antonio, 32
Lopes, Antonio (gr), 38
Lopes, Antonio Lino (gr), 45
Lopes, Baltasar, 36
Lopes, Barbara, 7, 29
Lopes, Felipe, 30
Lopes, Francisco, 33, 39
Lopes, Jose Antonio (gr), 19, 48
Lopes, Jose Felipe Santiago (gr), 16
Lopes, Jose Ramon, 15
Lopes, Jose Ysabel (gr), 30
Lopes, Juan Antonio (gr), 51
Lopes, Juan Bautista (gr), 19
Lopes, Juan Christoval, 16
Lopes, Juan Cristobal, 48
Lopes, Juan Rafael (gr), 15
Lopes, Juana Maria (br), 36
Lopes, Maria Barbara, 41, 52
Lopes, Maria de la Lus, 43
Lopes, Maria Dolores, 1, 11, 33, 44, 55
Lopes, Maria Dolores (br), 31
Lopes, Maria Gertrudis, 8
Lopes, Maria Jesusa, 3
Lopes, Maria Josefa (br), 41
Lopes, Maria Justafina, 46
Lopes, Maria Manuela, 51
Lopes, Maria Manuela (br), 15
Lopes, Maria Micaela, 12
Lopes, Maria Paula (br), 48

Lopes, Maria Rufina, 37, 42
Lopes, Maria Ruperta, 41
Lopes, Maria Serafina (br), 8
Lopes, Maria Teodora (br), 2
Lopes, Miguel, 8, 19, 41, 48
Lopes, Miguel Antonio, 3
Lopes, Pablo, 15
Lopes, Pedro, 33
Lopes, Ramon, 2, 17, 19, 30, 45
Lopes, Ramon Candelario (gr), 3
Lopes, Valtazar, 38
Lopes, Vitorina, 9
Lopes, Ysabel, 17
Lopez, Antonio Simon (gr), 43
Lopez, Juan Cristobal, 43
Lopez, Maria Dolores, 31
Lopez, Maria Gertrudes, 23
Lovato, Felipe Antonio (gr), 18
Lovato, Juan Pedro, 3
Lovato, Maria Manuela (br), 3
Lovato, Pedro Antonio, 4, 9
Lucero, Anamaria, 3
Lucero, Antonio Domingo, 28, 45, 46
Lucero, Antonio Domingo (gr), 21
Lucero, Antonio Jose (gr), 40
Lucero, Bibiana, 46
Lucero, Concepcion (gr), 2
Lucero, Consepcion, 50
Lucero, Cristobal, 26
Lucero, Diego Antonio, 4
Lucero, Encarnacion, 40
Lucero, Estefana, 17
Lucero, Faustina, 35
Lucero, Gregorio, 16, 21, 49
Lucero, Guadalupe, 15
Lucero, Jesus Maria, 44
Lucero, Jose Dolores (gr), 41
Lucero, Jose Francisco, 40
Lucero, Jose Maria (gr), 21, 49
Lucero, Jose Venedito (gr), 56
Lucero, Juan Agustin, 36
Lucero, Juan Agustin (gr), 16
Lucero, Juan Antonio (gr), 28
Lucero, Juan de Dios (gr), 23
Lucero, Juan de Jesus, 13, 29, 50
Lucero, Juan del Carmel, 41

Lucero, Juan del Carmen, 56
Lucero, Juan Ysidro, 35
Lucero, Juana Josefa, 40
Lucero, Juana Rosalia (br), 21
Lucero, Julian, 21
Lucero, Lorenso, 5
Lucero, Manuel Antonio, 28
Lucero, Margarita, 35, 53
Lucero, Maria Antonia, 25, 44, 55
Lucero, Maria Biviana, 40, 46
Lucero, Maria Concepcion, 53, 56
Lucero, Maria de Jesus (br), 36
Lucero, Maria de la Lus, 38, 40, 46, 57
Lucero, Maria Dolores, 20, 28, 55
Lucero, Maria Encarnacion, 40
Lucero, Maria Encarnacion (br), 19
Lucero, Maria Estefana, 30, 57
Lucero, Maria Faustina, 49
Lucero, Maria Francisca (br), 20
Lucero, Maria Gertrudes, 54
Lucero, Maria Guadalupe, 53
Lucero, Maria Josefa, 26, 32
Lucero, Maria Josefa (br), 21
Lucero, Maria Juana, 47
Lucero, Maria Juana (br), 26
Lucero, Maria Loreta, 26
Lucero, Maria Luisa, 22
Lucero, Maria Nestora (br), 36
Lucero, Maria Rufina (br), 49
Lucero, Miguel, 21, 26
Lucero, Nemecio de Jesus (gr), 29
Lucero, Pablo, 4, 19, 30, 49
Lucero, Pedro Antonio, 2
Lucero, Policarpio Martin (gr), 26
Lucero, Ramon, 20, 21, 23, 24
Lucero, Ricardo, 33
Lucero, Rumalda, 51
Lucero, Vicente, 24, 36
Lucsero, Maria Manuela, 9
Lugan, Jose de Jesus (gr), 15
Lugan, Juan Cristobal, 35
Lugan, Maria Asencion, 8
Lugan, Maria del Carmen, 18
Lugan, Nieves, 15
Lugan, Pedro Leon (gr), 5
Lujan, Ana Maria, 35, 57

Lujan, Antonio Andres (gr), 22
Lujan, Candelario (gr), 38
Lujan, Juan Christobal (gr), 14
Lujan, Juan Cristobal, 39
Lujan, Juan Cristobal (gr), 24
Lujan, Manuel, 22
Lujan, Maria Antonia, 49
Lujan, Maria Candelaria (br), 20
Lujan, Maria de Jesus, 1
Lujan, Maria del Carmel, 27
Lujan, Maria Dolores, 54
Lujan, Maria Gregorio, 34
Lujan, Maria Manuela, 3, 39
Lujan, Necolas, 38
Lujan, Nicolas, 24
Lujan, Pedro Leon, 20, 21, 26, 27, 48, 51
Lujan, Pedro Luis, 30
Lujan, Salbador, 14
Lujan, Vicente (gr), 54
Luna, Diego de, 9, 21, 50
Luna, Francisco Esteban Garcia de (gr), 5
Luna, Juan de, 14
Luna, Juan de (gr), 53
Luna, Juan de Jesus de, 32
Luna, Juana de, 5
Luna, Maria Encarnacion de (br), 32
Luna, Pablo de, 53
Luna, Ramon, 15
Luna, Viviana de, 23, 31
Lusero, Barbara, 11
Lusero, Encarnacion, 17
Lusero, Encarnacion (br), 9
Lusero, Guadalupe, 11, 14
Lusero, Juan de Jesus, 7, 14
Lusero, Manuel, 9, 11
Lusero, Margarita, 18
Lusero, Maria Guadalupe, 43
Lusero, Maria Guadalupe (br), 7
Lusero, Maria Matilde, 10
Lusero, Maria Ygnaca, 4
Lusero, Miguel, 7
Lusero, Nicolas, 33
Lusero, Santos, 11
Lusero, Vibiana, 34
Lusero, Vicente (gr), 11
Luzero, Maria Rumalda, 4

M

Madrid, Antonio, 39
Madrid, Antonio Jose, 7
Madrid, Bernardo, 17
Madrid, Casimiro (gr), 7
Madrid, Christoval, 15
Madrid, Cristobal, 33
Madrid, Diego, 7, 12, 15, 36, 38, 46
Madrid, Domingo (gr), 7
Madrid, Francisca, 4
Madrid, Ines, 52
Madrid, Jose Alejandro (gr), 39
Madrid, Jose Antonio, 3, 11
Madrid, Jose Domingo (gr), 16
Madrid, Jose Manuel (gr), 45
Madrid, Jose Miguel (gr), 17
Madrid, Jose Rafael, 49
Madrid, Juan, 29
Madrid, Juan Cristobal, 42
Madrid, Juan Salbador (gr), 29
Madrid, Julian, 2, 14, 24, 28
Madrid, Maria Antonia, 28
Madrid, Maria Antonia (br), 38
Madrid, Maria Beguina (br), 42
Madrid, Maria de la Luz, 30
Madrid, Maria Josefa (br), 49
Madrid, Maria Thomasa (br), 14
Madrid, Maria Ygnacia (br), 11
Madrid, Maria Ygnes (br), 25
Madrid, Micaela (br), 33
Madrid, Miguel, 28, 52
Madrid, Miguel Antonio, 38
Madrid, Miguel Antonio (gr), 28
Madrid, Miguel Antono, 45
Madrid, Pedro Antonio (gr), 28
Madrid, Reyes, 7
Madrid, Rosalia, 15
Madrid, Salvador, 25
Madrid, Savaldor, 16
Madrid, Ysavel (br), 52
Madril, Cristobal, 52
Madril, Juan Rafael (gr), 52
Madril, Juan Ysidro (gr), 56
Madril, Miguel, 56
Maes, Antonio (gr), 53

Maes, Antonio Bibian (gr), 51
Maes, Candelaria, 49
Maes, Gabriel, 51
Maes, Jose Maria (gr), 47
Maes, Juan Manuel, 35, 45, 46, 55
Maes, Juana Teresa de Jesus (br), 55
Maes, Maria Albina, 57
Maes, Maria Antonia, 3
Maes, Maria Antonia Encarnacion, 25
Maes, Maria Dolores, 15, 23, 40, 46
Maes, Maria Juliana, 36
Maes, Maria Juliana (br), 11
Maes, Maria Manuela, 46
Maes, Maria Martina (br), 46
Maes, Maria Miquela (br), 45
Maes, Maria Soledad (br), 58
Maes, Maria Vitalia, 19
Maes, Pedro, 47
Maes, Salbador, 11
Maes, Santiago, 53, 58
Maes, Vicente Ferrer, 4
Maese, Jose Pascual (gr), 32
Maese, Maria Manuela, 33
Maese, Maria Paula, 32
Maestas, Jose Antonio, 14
Maestas, Jose Maria, 6
Maestas, Juan Francisco (gr), 14
Maestas, Maria Casilda, 11
Maez, Maria Francisca, 2
Manasares, Jose Antonio, 29
Manasares, Maria Manuela (br), 29
Manchego, Jose Francisco, 42
Manchego, Jose Francisco (gr), 42
Manchego, Jose Manuel, 22
Manchego, Manuel Estevan, 30
Manchego, Maria Manuela (br), 30
Manchego, Maria Paula, 47
Manchego, Ramon (gr), 22
Mansanares, Ana Maria, 6
Mansanares, Ana Maria (br), 27
Mansanares, Antonio, 28, 51
Mansanares, Jose Antonio, 30, 38
Mansanares, Jose Manuel (gr), 22
Mansanares, Jose Rumaldo (gr), 30
Mansanares, Josefa, 6, 9, 23
Mansanares, Juan Andres (gr), 30

Mansanares, Manuel, 7, 14, 22, 30
Mansanares, Manuel Antonio, 27
Mansanares, Manuel Gregorio, 6
Mansanares, Maria Francisca, 31
Mansanares, Maria Gertrudis, 45
Mansanares, Maria Josefa, 45
Mansanares, Maria Juana, 35, 51
Mansanares, Maria Rafela, 51
Mansanares, Pedro Nolasco (gr), 14
Manzanares, Francisco (gr), 1
Manzanares, Juan Cristobal, 1
Mares, Antonio Manzanarez, 34
Marques, Diego, 18
Marques, Jose Vicente (gr), 18
Marques, Manuel, 8, 11, 12
Marques, Maria Barbara (br), 8
Marques, Maria de la Luz, 48
Marques, Maria Guadalupe (br), 53
Marques, Maria Manuela, 40
Marques, Maria Manuela (br), 11
Marques, Maria Miquela, 18
Marques, Miguel Antonio (gr), 10
Marques, Vicente, 53
Martin, Acencion, Maria de la, 22
Martin, Agapito (gr), 49
Martin, Altagracia, 50
Martin, Anamaria, 13
Martin, Antonio, 2, 4, 6, 8, 9, 11, 17, 18, 20, 21, 22, 25, 34
Martin, Antonio de Jesus, 13
Martin, Antonio de Jesus (gr), 11
Martin, Asencion, 14
Martin, Baltsar, 50
Martin, Bibiana, 4
Martin, Buenabentura, 39
Martin, Christobal, 6, 13, 15
Martin, Cristobal, 1, 21, 24, 48
Martin, Dolores, 12
Martin, Domingo, 1, 2, 3, 5, 6, 10, 12, 13, 15, 16, 21
Martin, Estefana, 20
Martin, Eusebio, 45
Martin, Faustina (br), 22
Martin, Felipe, 43, 50
Martin, Felipe (gr), 25
Martin, Fernando, 38

Martin, Francisca, 39
Martin, Francisco, 2, 17, 25, 35, 49, 51
Martin, Francisco (gr), 6, 7
Martin, Francisco Antonio, 9
Martin, Francisco Antonio (gr), 23, 49
Martin, Francisco Estevan (gr), 10
Martin, Gregorio, 41
Martin, Guadalupe, 5, 23, 50
Martin, Jesus Maria, 11, 50
Martin, Jesus Maria (gr), 21
Martin, Joaquin, 26
Martin, Jose, 1, 2, 8, 10, 13, 17, 20, 21, 23, 25
Martin, Jose Aniseto (gr), 49
Martin, Jose Antonio, 12, 13, 18, 50
Martin, Jose Antonio (gr), 6, 22
Martin, Jose Benito (gr), 20
Martin, Jose Cristoval, 1
Martin, Jose Eucebio (gr), 1
Martin, Jose Francisco, 50
Martin, Jose Julian, 2, 6
Martin, Jose Julian (gr), 4
Martin, Jose Manuel, 26, 31, 45, 46, 49
Martin, Jose Maria, 45
Martin, Jose Maria (gr), 17, 21, 25
Martin, Jose Mariano (gr), 15
Martin, Jose Ramon, 26
Martin, Jose Santiago (gr), 21
Martin, Jose Teodoro (gr), 50
Martin, Juan, 3, 16, 48, 50
Martin, Juan Antonio (gr), 1, 18
Martin, Juan de Dios, 7, 15, 25
Martin, Juan de Jesus, 6
Martin, Juan de Jesus (gr), 8
Martin, Juan Domingo, 5, 10, 15, 20
Martin, Juan Francisco, 7
Martin, Juan Jose, 24
Martin, Juan Manuel, 14, 50
Martin, Juan Pascual, 47
Martin, Juan Pasqual (gr), 4
Martin, Juan Pedro, 7, 11
Martin, Juan Rosalio, 6, 8
Martin, Juan Simon, 12, 16
Martin, Juan Ygnacio (gr), 41
Martin, Juana, 7, 18, 23, 49
Martin, Juana Gertrudis (br), 1

Martin, Juana Manuela, 11
Martin, Juana Maria, 51
Martin, Julian, 8, 49
Martin, Loreta, 41
Martin, Manuel, 1, 22, 29
Martin, Manuel (gr), 13
Martin, Manuel Antonio (gr), 27
Martin, Manuel Gregorio, 2, 15
Martin, Manuel Lorenzo, 1, 3, 22
Martin, Manuel Rafael, 9
Martin, Manuel Rafael (gr), 1
Martin, Manuela, 6, 17
Martin, Margarita, 13
Martin, Margarita Solome (br), 33
Martin, Maria Acencion, 22
Martin, Maria Aniseta (br), 49
Martin, Maria Antonia, 4, 13, 29, 33, 36, 41, 48
Martin, Maria Antonia (br), 14, 32
Martin, Maria Ascencion, 27
Martin, Maria Barbara, 24
Martin, Maria Barbara (br), 10, 18
Martin, Maria Bibiana (br), 16, 19
Martin, Maria Candelaria, 10, 17, 23
Martin, Maria Candelaria (br), 11
Martin, Maria Cerafina de los Angeles, 12
Martin, Maria Concepcion, 5
Martin, Maria Consepcion (br), 13
Martin, Maria de Jesus, 4, 44, 51
Martin, Maria de Jesus (br), 1, 15
Martin, Maria de la Lus, 7, 10, 11, 21, 27
Martin, Maria de la Lus (br), 26
Martin, Maria de la Luz, 12, 26, 37
Martin, Maria de Refugio, 7
Martin, Maria Decideria (br), 34
Martin, Maria Dolores, 1, 2, 7, 41
Martin, Maria Dolores (br), 15, 23
Martin, Maria Elena, 25
Martin, Maria Encarnacion, 5
Martin, Maria Encarnacion (br), 17
Martin, Maria Estefana, 26
Martin, Maria Francisca, 1, 32
Martin, Maria Francisca (br), 43
Martin, Maria Getrudes, 13
Martin, Maria Getrudis, 9
Martin, Maria Guadalupe, 32

Martin, Maria Guadalupe (br), 13, 18, 43, 50
Martin, Maria Josefa, 3, 10, 12, 14, 19, 33
Martin, Maria Josefa (br), 6, 10, 47
Martin, Maria Juana, 12, 23, 47, 48
Martin, Maria Juana **(br)**, 50
Martin, Maria Juana Antonia, 39
Martin, Maria Juana Gertrudis, 48
Martin, Maria Juliana Gracia (br), 21
Martin, Maria Loreta, 47
Martin, Maria Manuel, 37
Martin, Maria Manuela, 1, 6, 7, 20, 24, 50
Martin, Maria Manuela (br), 7
Martin, Maria Margarita **(br)**, 49
Martin, Maria Marina Romana (br), 1
Martin, Maria Mauricia, 47, 51
Martin, Maria Maurina, 35
Martin, Maria Miguela de la Crus, 31
Martin, Maria Pasquala, 16, 18
Martin, Maria Pasquela, 8
Martin, Maria Paubla, 12, 15
Martin, Maria Rafaela, 27
Martin, Maria Rafaela (br), 3, 13, 22, 50
Martin, Maria Rosa, 41
Martin, Maria Rosa (br), 24
Martin, Maria Roza, 5
Martin, Maria Rufina (br), 8
Martin, Maria Rutila (br), 6
Martin, Maria Santa (br), 5
Martin, Maria Sencion, 31
Martin, Maria Soledad, 2, 31
Martin, Maria Soledad **(br)**, 50
Martin, Maria Teodora (br), 7, 50
Martin, Maria Tomasa, 10, 22
Martin, Maria Toribia, 3, 10
Martin, Maria Ygnacia, 28, 35
Martin, Maria Ygnes, 6, 46, 49
Martin, Maria Ynes (br), 4
Martin, Maria Ysabel, 6
Martin, Maria Ysabel (br), 14, 16, 31
Martin, Maria Ysabel Teodora (br), 33
Martin, Martin de Jesus, 3, 6, 20
Martin, Miguel, 37, 39, 40, 44, 49, 51
Martin, Nicolasa, 48
Martin, Pablo, 20, 23, 33
Martin, Pascuala, 18

Martin, Pasquala, 26
Martin, Patricia, 24
Martin, Patrocinia, 13
Martin, Paublo, 8
Martin, Pedro, 9, 14, 50
Martin, Pedro Antonio, 18
Martin, Pedro Antonio (gr), 16, 25
Martin, Pedro Jose (gr), 39
Martin, Rafael, 21
Martin, Ramon, 9, 12, 15, 16, 22, 23, 24, 49
Martin, Santiago, 6, 27, 32
Martin, Seberino, 4
Martin, Seferino, 49
Martin, Serafina, 13, 21
Martin, Silveria, 17
Martin, Simon, 51
Martin, Sisto, 11
Martin, Tomas, 21
Martin, Tomasa (br), 8
Martin, Valtasar (gr), 29
Martin, Ygnacio, 18
Martin, Ysidro, 3, 5, 9, 14, 39
Martines, Agapito (gr), 31
Martines, Agustin (gr), 40
Martines, Albino, 48
Martines, Ana Maria, 54
Martines, Antonio, 31, 32
Martines, Antonio Domingo, 31
Martines, Antonio Jose (gr), 27, 52
Martines, Antonio Jose Ramaldo (gr), 29
Martines, Candelaria, 29
Martines, Carmen, 51
Martines, Cristobal, 37, 52
Martines, Diego Antonio (gr), 47
Martines, Encarnacion, 52
Martines, Esteban, 40
Martines, Estefana, 37
Martines, Eusebio, 32
Martines, Felipe, 34, 57
Martines, Felipe de Jesus, 56
Martines, Fernandes (gr), 45
Martines, Francisco, 35, 52
Martines, Francisco Antonio (gr), 48
Martines, Gertrudis, 28
Martines, Guadalupe, 34
Martines, Hermenegildo (gr), 53

Martines, Jesus Manuel, 43
Martines, Jesus Maria (gr), 50
Martines, Jose, 29, 31
Martines, Jose Alvino, 30
Martines, Jose Andres (gr), 46
Martines, Jose de Jesus (gr), 52
Martines, Jose Deciderio (gr), 53
Martines, Jose Francisco, 34
Martines, Jose Francisco (gr), 55
Martines, Jose Julian, 46
Martines, Jose Manuel, 47, 53, 54, 55, 56, 57, 58
Martines, Jose Manuel (gr), 30
Martines, Jose Maria, 36, 47
Martines, Jose Miguel (gr), 29
Martines, Jose Pablo (gr), 47
Martines, Jose Romuelo de Jesus (gr), 56
Martines, Juan Antonio, 53
Martines, Juan Cristobal, 31
Martines, Juan de Dios (gr), 54
Martines, Juan de Jesus (gr), 54
Martines, Juan del Rosario, 45
Martines, Juan Jose, 27, 29, 52
Martines, Juan Manuel, 53, 56
Martines, Juan Miguel, 43, 54
Martines, Juana, 53
Martines, Julian, 32, 45
Martines, Manuel, 19, 55
Martines, Manuel Rafael, 43
Martines, Manuel Rafael (gr), 44
Martines, Maria, 56
Martines, Maria Agapita (br), 29
Martines, Maria Altagracia, 38
Martines, Maria Antonia, 36
Martines, Maria Bernardina, 35
Martines, Maria Biviana, 38
Martines, Maria de Jesus, 28, 29
Martines, Maria de Jesus (br), 37
Martines, Maria de la Lus, 28, 35, 44
Martines, Maria de la Luz, 32
Martines, Maria de los Reyes, 58
Martines, Maria del Carmel, 34, 43
Martines, Maria del Refugio, 45
Martines, Maria Dolores, 37, 46, 57
Martines, Maria Dolores **(br)**, 47
Martines, Maria Doretea (br), 43

Martines, Maria Encarnacion (br), 38
Martines, Maria Francisca, 42
Martines, Maria Josefa, 29, 30, 49
Martines, Maria Juana (br), 46
Martines, Maria Juana Rosalia (br), 45
Martines, Maria Juanita (br), 30
Martines, Maria Leonora (br), 36
Martines, Maria Manuela, 30, 36, 45, 50, 52, 55, 57
Martines, Maria Margarita (br), 32
Martines, Maria Monica, 55
Martines, Maria Pelegrina (br), 29
Martines, Maria Policarpio (br), 57
Martines, Maria Rafaela (br), 54
Martines, Maria Regina (br), 43
Martines, Maria Rosa (br), 47, 56
Martines, Maria Seferina (br), 48
Martines, Maria Simona (br), 56
Martines, Maria Soledad, 34
Martines, Maria Trinidad (br), 32
Martines, Maria Victoria, 45
Martines, Maria Ygnacia, 42
Martines, Maria Ygnacio, 49
Martines, Maria Ygnes, 28
Martines, Maria Ynes, 39
Martines, Maria Ynes (br), 52
Martines, Martin, 28
Martines, Mauricia, 51
Martines, Miguela de Jesus, 57
Martines, Nicolas, 55
Martines, Pedro Antonio, 47, 49
Martines, Pedro Ygnacio (gr), 35
Martines, Ramon, 46
Martines, Reyes, 53
Martines, Seberino, 35
Martines, Simon (gr), 34
Martines, Ygnacio, 31
Martines, Ysidro Pancario, 48
Martinez, Baltazar, 42
Martinez, Jose Manuel (gr), 33
Martinez, Julian, 33
Martinez, Manuel Gregorio (gr), 42
Martinez, Maria Altagracia, 32
Martinez, Maria de Jesus, 29
Martinez, Maria del Carmel, 41
Martinez, Maria Teodora, 52

Martinez, Maria Ysabel (br), 31
Mascareñas, Maria de Jesus, 9
Mascareñas, Maria de la Lus, 48
Mascareñas, Maria Magdalena, 33
Masquareñas, Mariana, 10
Mastas, Maria Francisca, 9
Medina, Diego, 13
Medina, Gregorio, 19
Medina, Jose Cipriano (gr), 13
Medina, Jose Pablo, 18
Medina, Juan Nepomuceno (gr), 56
Medina, Maria Luisa, 1
Medina, Maria Luzia, 27
Medina, Maria Manuela (br), 19
Medina, Ygnacio, 56
Mejicano, Antonio Jose (gr), 13
Mejicano, Ysidro, 13
Mes, Benigno (gr), 35
Mes, Maria Manuela, 33
Mestas, Bartolo, 48
Mestas, Candelaria, 49
Mestas, Carmen, 55
Mestas, Casilda, 9
Mestas, Feliciano, 24
Mestas, Francisco Antonio (gr), 42
Mestas, Jose Antonio, 4
Mestas, Jose Antonio (gr), 15
Mestas, Jose Maria, 42
Mestas, Jose Maria del Carmen, 11
Mestas, Jose Mariano (gr), 11
Mestas, Juan de Jesus (gr), 48
Mestas, Juan Simon, 8
Mestas, Luis, 15, 23
Mestas, Maria Aguida de Jesus, 56
Mestas, Maria Antonia, 23
Mestas, Maria Bartola (br), 55
Mestas, Maria Candelaria, 43
Mestas, Maria Candelaria (br), 49
Mestas, Maria Casilda, 28
Mestas, Maria Clara, 46
Mestas, Maria del Rosario, 22
Mestas, Maria Dolores (br), 24
Mestas, Maria Francisca, 10, 38
Mestas, Maria Luteria (br), 6
Mestas, Maria Luysa (br), 30
Mestas, Maria Manuela, 8, 24, 41, 42, 48

Mestas, Maria Perfecta (br), 23
Mestas, Maria Rita (br), 8
Mestas, Maria Rosalia, 19, 37
Mestas, Maria Rutila, 50
Mestas, Maria Victoria, 46
Mestas, Maria Ysabel, 30
Mestas, Miguel, 49
Mestas, Miguel Antonio (gr), 4
Mestas, Rafael, 48
Mestes, Maria Lucia, 9
Mez, Maria, 18
Miera, Antonio, 3, 12
Miera, Maria Estefana (br), 12
Molina, Juana (br), 24
Molina, Lorenso, 24
Molina, Maria Josefa (br), 18
Mondragon, Maria Felipa, 25
Mondragon, Maria Manuela, 14
Montaño, Faustin, 5, 6
Montaño, Faustino, 26
Montaño, Fernando, 13, 43, 44, 45, 46, 51
Montaño, Francisco, 13
Moñtano, Francisco, 24
Montaño, Joae Maria, 45
Montaño, Jose Fernando (gr), 13, 55
Montaño, Jose Maria, 38, 43, 44, 45, 46, 55
Montaño, Jose Tomas, 46
Montaño, Maria, 38
Montaño, Maria del Jesus, 48
Montaño, Maria Guadalupe (br), 51
Montaño, Maria Josefa (br), 26
Montaño, Maria Manuela, 30
Montaño, Maria Rosa, 30
Montaño, Maria Rosa del Pilar, 46
Montaño, Melquiades Antonio, 30
Montaño, Vicente S., 30
Montolla, Barbara, 7
Montolla, Jose Secilio (gr), 35
Montolla, Marcial, 11
Montolla, Maria de la Lus, 35
Montolla, Rosalia, 11
Montoya, Barbara, 5, 9, 14, 15
Montoya, Bibian (gr), 34
Montoya, Cristobal (gr), 23
Montoya, Diego, 14
Montoya, Fernando, 57

Montoya, Fernando de, 39
Montoya, Gregorio, 39
Montoya, Jose Manuel, 24
Montoya, Josefa, 26
Montoya, Juan Pablo Antonio (gr), 25
Montoya, Juan Vicente, 25
Montoya, Manuel, 1, 17
Montoya, Maria Arcadia, 55
Montoya, Maria Cararima, 23
Montoya, Maria Catarina, 37
Montoya, Maria Comcepcion, 38
Montoya, Maria Cristesna (br), 17
Montoya, Maria de la Lus, 14
Montoya, Maria Josefa, 27
Montoya, Maria Juliana, 35
Montoya, Maria Juliana Gracia (br), 24
Montoya, Maria Rosalia, 34
Montoya, Maria Teodora, 20
Montoya, Maria Ygnacia (br), 39
Montoya, Nerio (gr), 57
Montoya, Theodora, 15
Moreno, Antonio, 34
Moreno, Francisco (gr), 34
Moya, Ana Maria, 16
Moya, Antonio Jose, 8
Moya, Joaquina, 8
Moya, Jose, 13
Moya, Jose Ygnacio (gr), 8
Moya, Juan de Dios (gr), 13
Moya, Maria Bibiana (br), 34
Moya, Maria Concepcion, 34
Moya, Maria Gertrudes, 23
Moya, Maria Josefa, 15, 42, 52
Muñis, Bernardo, 5, 7, 9, 15
Muñis, Mariana, 9
Muños, Antonio, 7, 8, 12, 16
Muños, Bernardo, 14
Muños, Jose, 50
Muños, Jose Antonio Sebastian (gr), 12
Muños, Soledad, 28

N

Naranjo, Antonia Visenta, 13
Naranjo, Diego, 32
Naranjo, Felipe Neri (gr), 3

Naranjo, Josefa, 6
Naranjo, Maria de Jesus, 10
Naranjo, Maria de la Lus, 34
Naranjo, Maria de Lus, 12
Naranjo, Maria Dolores, 3
Naranjo, Maria Gregoria, 32
Naranjo, Maria Josefa, 26
Naranjo, Maria Juliana, 34
Naranjo, Maria Rumalda (br), 32
Naranjo, Nereo, 15
Naranjo, Noberto, 3, 24, 25, 32
Nieto, Maria Francisca, 20
Noriega, Jose, 20
Noriega, Jose Maria de (gr), 37
Noriega, Jose Miguel de, 37
Noriega, Maria Agueda (br), 20

O

Ocaña, Julian, 11, 45, 54
Ocaña, Luis (gr), 54
Ocaña, Maria Francisca (br), 54
Ocana, Rafael, 51
Ocano, Aquilino, 41
Olgin, Christobal, 8
Olgin, Consecion, 8
Olgin, Consepcion, 12
Olgin, Francisca, 22
Olgin, Juan, 6, 18
Olgin, Juan Jose, 3, 11
Olgin, Maria Dolores, 6
Olgin, Maria Soledad (br), 8
Olguin, Juan Jose, 3, 22
Olguin, Antonio Jose, 33
Olguin, Cristobal, 19, 25
Olguin, Francisca, 19
Olguin, Francisco Antonio (gr), 19
Olguin, Jesus Maria (gr), 33
Olguin, Maria Dolores, 40
Olguin, Maria Francisca, 32
Olguin, Maria Joaquina, 34
Olguin, Maria Manuela, 27
Olguin, Maria Trinidad (br), 19, 25
Olguin, Ygnacia, 50
Olibari, Juan de Dios, 34
Olibas, Maria Manuela, 44

Olivas, Jose Santiago (gr), 14
Olivas, Juan de Carmen, 14
Olivas, Maria Josefa, 43
Ortega, Anna Maria, 35
Ortega, Antonio, 37, 46, 47
Ortega, Jose Antonio, 19
Ortega, Juan, 46
Ortega, Juan Ygnacio, 18, 19
Ortega, Maria de Jesus (br), 19
Ortega, Maria del Carmel, 15
Ortega, Maria del Carmen, 31
Ortega, Maria Yisdora, 24
Ortega, Pedro Antonio de Esquipula (gr), 46
Ortega, Ysidora, 36
Ortis, Antonio, 31, 45
Ortis, Catarida, 32
Ortis, Geronima, 56
Ortis, Guadalupe, 21
Ortis, Juan (gr), 39
Ortis, Maria de la Crus, 22
Ortis, Maria Manuela, 33
Ortis, Maria Salome, 40
Ortis, Salbador, 39
Ortiz, Agustin, 3
Ortiz, Antonio Eugenio (gr), 8
Ortiz, Caterina, 8
Ortiz, Don Jose Maria, 1
Ortiz, Doña Ysadora, 1
Ortiz, Esteban, 8
Ortiz, Marcos, 5
Ortiz, Maria Catarina, 33
Ortiz, Maria Josefa, 5
Ortiz, Rafael, 16
Ortiz. Jose Maria del Socorro, 13

P

Pacheco, Maria Loreta, 24
Padilla, Alejandro, 39
Padilla, Maria de los Angeles (br), 35
Padilla, Maria Rosa, 7
Padilla, Maria Ygnacia (br), 39
Padilla, Santo, 35
Paes, Maria Juliana, 4
Paes, Victoria, 5

Pando, Caldelario, 51
Pando, Maria Manuela, 3
Pando, Maria Petra (br), 51
Pando, Maria Rita, 10
Patrona, Juana Getrudes, 7
Peña, Antonio Serafin (gr), 33
Peña, Felipe Santiago (gr), 24
Peña, Juan Antonio (gr), 57
Peña, Juana Maria de Jesus, 8
Peña, Manuel, 19
Peña, Maria Manuela (br), 45
Peña, Mariano, 33
Peña, Mariano (gr), 19
Peña, Pedro, 8, 24, 33
Peña, Rafael, 45, 57
Prieto, Antonio, 26

Q

Quintana, Agustin, 20
Quintana, Antonia Getrudis, 55
Quintana, Antonio Jose (gr), 9
Quintana, Baltasar, 6, 22
Quintana, Biviana, 57
Quintana, Brigida, 49
Quintana, Esquipula, 56
Quintana, Feliciana, 57
Quintana, Gregorio (gr), 57
Quintana, Jesus, 21
Quintana, Jose Antonio, 17, 35, 57
Quintana, Jose de la Cruz (gr), 56
Quintana, Jose Guadalupe (gr), 21
Quintana, Juan Andres (gr), 44
Quintana, Juan Antonio (gr), 13
Quintana, Juan de Jesus, 13
Quintana, Juan Domingo, 35
Quintana, Juana, 3
Quintana, Manuel, 41
Quintana, Maria Altagracia, 48
Quintana, Maria Antonia, 7, 25, 32, 40, 51
Quintana, Maria Antonia (br), 6
Quintana, Maria Bibiana (br), 14
Quintana, Maria Candelaria (br), 35
Quintana, Maria de Esquipula (br), 20
Quintana, Maria de la Lus, 18, 39, 53
Quintana, Maria Francisca, 12

Quintana, Maria Juana, 48
Quintana, Maria Juliana (br), 41
Quintana, Maria Manuela, 1, 22
Quintana, Maria Margarita, 28
Quintana, Miguel, 14, 44, 56
Quintana, Polonia, 25

R

Rael, Maria Guadalupe, 17, 21
Ramires, Juana Maria, 37
Ramires, Maria Juana, 20
Ramires, Miguel, 8
Ribera, Antonio Jose, 51
Ribera, Guadalupe, 49
Ribera, Jose Manuel, 6
Ribera, Maria Antonia, 36
Ribera, Maria Dolores, 45
Ribera, Maria Manuela (br), 45
Rivera, Jose Francisco (gr), 23
Rivera, Juan de Dios, 23
Rivera, Maria Antonia, 26
Rodriges, Maria Dolores, 11
Rodriges, Maria Francisca, 6
Rodriges, Maria Paubla, 18
Rodriges, Paubla, 6, 11
Rodrigues, Diego, 48
Rodrigues, Diego (gr), 48
Rodrigues, Francisco, 53
Rodrigues, Jose Rafael, 5, 35
Rodrigues, Juana Maria (br), 53
Rodrigues, Maria Dolores, 6, 42
Rodrigues, Maria Paula, 3
Rodrigues, Martia Rugina (br), 35
Roibal, Juan Luis del Refugio (gr), 21
Roibal, Maria Guadalupe, 21
Roibal, Maria Josefa, 19
Roibal, Maria Paubla, 53
Roibal, Tomas, 21, 25
Roival, Maria Guadalupe, 13
Romero, Antonia Rosa, 20, 26, 48
Romero, Francisco, 31, 33
Romero, Francisco (gr), 41
Romero, Guadalupe, 41
Romero, Jose Antonio, 1
Romero, Jose Miguel, 21, 47

Romero, Jose Tomas, 47
Romero, Jose Tomas (gr), 33
Romero, Jose Ygnacio (gr), 24
Romero, Juan Antonio (gr), 32
Romero, Juan de Jesus (gr), 31
Romero, Juan Francisco, 24
Romero, Juana (br), 25
Romero, Luis, 4
Romero, Manuel Antonio (gr), 47
Romero, Maria Antonia, 18
Romero, Maria Antonia Rosa, 36
Romero, Maria Concepcion, 20, 33
Romero, Maria del Refugio (br), 38
Romero, Maria del Rosario, 35
Romero, Maria Dolores, 24, 51
Romero, Maria Guadalupe, 43
Romero, Maria Juana, 43
Romero, Maria Juliana (br), 35
Romero, Maria Manuela, 29
Romero, Maria Paula, 34
Romero, Maria Soledad, 15, 24
Romero, Maria Tomasa, 39, 51
Romero, Maria Tomasa Casimira (br), 4
Romero, Maria Ygnacia, 16, 21
Romero, Maria Ysabel, 19
Romero, Miguel Antonio, 24
Romero, Pablo, 7, 23, 38
Romero, Petrona, 21
Romero, Ramon, 24
Romero, Rosita (br), 1
Romero, Santos, 25
Romero, Soledad, 38
Romero, Tomas, 32, 35
Romo, Nicolasa, 53
Roybal, Maria Paula, 56
Rubali, Maria Juliana, 45
Ruibal, Antonio, 50
Ruibal, Consecion, 6
Ruibal, Francisco Estevan (gr), 31
Ruibal, Jose, 33
Ruibal, Jose Francisco, 40
Ruibal, Jose Miguel, 29
Ruibal, Juan de Dios (gr), 50
Ruibal, Maria Casimira Ramona (br), 14
Ruibal, Maria Francisa, 40
Ruibal, Maria Francisca, 41, 44

Ruibal, Maria Juliana (br), 8
Ruibal, Maria Liodocia (br), 33
Ruibal, Thomas, 14
Ruibal, Tomas de Jesus, 31
Ruibali, Ana Maria de los Dolores (br), 22
Ruibali, Antonio Romaldo (gr), 23
Ruibali, Juan Antonio, 22
Ruibali, Juan de Jesus, 18
Ruibali, Maria de la Lus (br), 26
Ruibali, Maria Dolores (br), 26
Ruibali, Maria Francisca, 37, 39
Ruibali, Maria Josefa (br), 54
Ruibali, Maria Luisa, 4
Ruibali, Maria Manuela, 25
Ruibali, Maria Marselina, 39
Ruibali, Maria Paubla, 55
Ruibali, Maria Paula, 2
Ruibali, Marselina, 37
Ruibali, Ramon, 1, 26
Ruis, Jose Gregorio, 38
Ruis, Maria Candelaria (br), 48
Ruis, Maria Guadalupe, 38
Ruis, Rafael, 48
Ruivali, Juan de Jesus, 3
Ruivali, Juan de Jesus (gr), 3
Ruivali, Maria Candelaria, 3
Ruivibali, Maria Marcelina, 46

S

Salas, Antonio Maria, 47
Salas, Antonio Maria (gr), 31
Salas, Diego, 52
Salas, Jose Rafael, 31, 57
Salas, Maria Concepcion (br), 57
Salas, Maria de la Lus (br), 56
Salas, Maria del Carmen, 11, 17
Salas, Maria Gertrudes, 20
Salas, Maria Gregoria (br), 51
Salas, Maria Juana, 56
Salas, Maria Rosa, 53
Salasar, Andres, 39, 47
Salasar, Antonio J., 35
Salasar, Antonio Jesus (gr), 29
Salasar, Antonio Jose, 34
Salasar, Candelaria, 41

Salasar, Consepcion, 49
Salasar, Esquipula, 54
Salasar, Estefania, 11
Salasar, Francisco, 33, 36, 38, 42
Salasar, Francisco Antonio, 26
Salasar, Francisco Antonio (gr), 44
Salasar, Jesus Maria (gr), 51
Salasar, Jose, 29
Salasar, Jose Benito (gr), 31
Salasar, Jose Domingo (gr), 52
Salasar, Jose Francisco (gr), 26
Salasar, Jose Manuel, 11, 13, 29, 32
Salasar, Jose Miguel, 20, 30
Salasar, Jose Ygnacio, 35
Salasar, Jose Ygnacio (gr), 24
Salasar, Juan, 13, 16, 44, 48, 49
Salasar, Juan (gr), 32
Salasar, Juan Christobal, 13
Salasar, Juan de Jesus (gr), 30
Salasar, Juan Felipe, 37
Salasar, Juana, 52
Salasar, Manuel, 25, 38, 41, 43
Salasar, Manuel de Esquipula (gr), 24
Salasar, Manuela, 16
Salasar, Manuela de, 16
Salasar, Maria Alcadia, 34
Salasar, Maria Asencion, 36
Salasar, Maria Benigna, 32
Salasar, Maria Biviana, 41
Salasar, Maria Catarina (br), 48
Salasar, Maria de Jesus, 25
Salasar, Maria de la Lus (br), 20, 25
Salasar, Maria de Las Ascencion, 24
Salasar, Maria Delubina, 38, 43
Salasar, Maria Delubina (br), 44
Salasar, Maria Dolores (br), 29, 48
Salasar, Maria Francisa, 29
Salasar, Maria Francisca (br), 29
Salasar, Maria Gertrudes, 22
Salasar, Maria Gertrudis, 11
Salasar, Maria Getrudes, 17
Salasar, Maria Getrudis, 17
Salasar, Maria Manuela (br), 37
Salasar, Maria Rosa, 42, 44
Salasar, Maria Rosa de los Reyes, 14
Salasar, Maria Rosa de los Reyes (br), 13

Salasar, Maria Rufina, 5
Salasar, Maria Rufina (br), 31, 54
Salasar, Maria Salome, 32
Salasar, Maria Serafina (br), 13
Salasar, Maria Soledad, 31, 34, 38, 39, 42
Salasar, Maria Ygnacia (br), 47
Salasar, Migel, 32
Salasar, Pedro, 44, 51
Salasar, Pedro Ygnacio (gr), 11
Salasar, Rufina, 49
Salasar, Sabino, 37, 42, 44, 46
Salasar, Salbador, 31
Salasar, Santiago, 24, 51
Salasar, Sebastian, 47
Salasar, Soledad, 47
Salasar, Tomas, 29
Salazar, Francisco Antonio, 21
Salazar, Jose Manuel, 2, 27
Salazar, Jose Ramon (gr), 2
Salazar, Manuel, 16
Salazar, Maria Alcadia, 7
Salazar, Maria de Jesus (br), 21
Salazar, Maria Manuela, 3
Salazar, Maria Nasarena, 24
Salazar, Maria Nestora (br), 2
Salazar, Maria Soledad (br), 16
Salazar, Ylario, 2
Samora, Encarnacion, 37
Samora, Francisco, 4
Samora, Josefa, 49
Samora, Juan, 3
Samora, Juan de Jesus, 37
Samora, Juan Santos (gr), 37
Samora, Juana Angela, 15
Samora, Maria Barbara, 11
Samora, Maria de la Cruz (br), 3
Samora, Maria Guadalupe (br), 37
Samora, Maria Josefa (br), 4
Samora, Maria Josefa de los Reyes, 3
Samora, Maria Paubla (br), 10
Samora, Maria Soledad (br), 54
Samora, Miguel, 54
Samora, Paula, 29
Samora, Rafaela, 25
Sanches, Alfonso, 56
Sanches, Antonia Rosalia, 9

Sanches, Antonio, 23
Sanches, Cararina del Refugio (br), 23
Sanches, Catarina, 9
Sanches, Guadalupe, 38, 42
Sanches, Jose Antonio, 9, 31
Sanches, Jose Manuel (gr), 31
Sanches, Jose Tomas (gr), 38
Sanches, Juan Andres, 16, 46
Sanches, Juan Manuel (gr), 14
Sanches, Maria Antonia, 14, 26, 29, 38, 48
Sanches, Maria Encarnacion, 36
Sanches, Maria Guadalupe, 29
Sanches, Maria Josefa, 34
Sanches, Maria Leonor (br), 46
Sanches, Maria Natividad (br), 47
Sanches, Maria Venigna de Jesus (br), 56
Sanches, Mariana, 29, 43, 44
Sanches, Natividad, 48
Sanches, Rafaela, 11
Sanches, Ramon, 38
Sanches, Ramos, 47
Sanches, Santiago, 14
Sanches, Soledad, 29
Sanches, Ylaria de Jesus, 4
Sanches, Ysidro Pasqual (gr), 4
Sanchez, Maria de la Lus, 36
Sandobal, Ana Maria (br), 53
Sandobal, Jose Francisco (gr), 35
Sandobal, Maria Faustina (br), 37
Sandobal, Maria Sencion, 30
Sandobal, Maria Serafina, 47
Sandobal, Salbador, 53
Sandobal, Viatris, 50
Sandoval, Maria Asencion, 14
Sandoval, Ysavel, 54
Santiestevan, Julian, 5
Santiestevan, Maria de la Luz (br), 5
Santiestevan, Maria del Carmel, 4
Santisteban, Santiago, 29
Seguaro, Eulogio (gr), 38
Segura, Jose Miguel, 24
Segura, Manuel, 10
Segura, Maria Consepcion (br), 10
Segura, Maria de Rosario, 41
Sena, Anamaria, 11
Sena, Juan de los Reyes, 2

Sena, Juan Reyes, 1
Sena, Maria de la Luz, 1
Sena, Maria de la Luz (br), 2
Sena, Maria Gertrudis, 48
Sena, Miguel Antonio (gr), 10
Serda, Antonio Jose (gr), 22
Serda, Antonio Jose de la (gr), 6
Serda, Diego Antonio (gr), 24
Serda, Domingo, 1, 6, 24
Serda, Jose Mariano (gr), 9
Serda, Maria Consepcion (br), 1
Serda, Maria de Jesus, 17
Serda, Maria Josefa, 16
Serrano, Hipolito, 42
Serrano, Jose, 10
Serrano, Jose Mariano, 31
Serrano, Juan Bautista (gr), 42
Serrano, Manuel, 41
Serrano, Manuel Gregorio (gr), 7
Serrano, Maria de Jesus (br), 41
Serrano, Maria Francisca, 12, 54
Serrano, Maria Francisca (br), 24
Serrano, Mariano, 12
Serrano, Mariano (gr), 24
Serrano, Ypolito, 7, 24
Sisneros, Alejadro, 32
Sisneros, Barbara, 21
Sisneros, Biviana, 2
Sisneros, Candelaria, 48
Sisneros, Catarina, 12
Sisneros, Encarnacion, 41
Sisneros, Francisca, 10, 13
Sisneros, Jose Gabriel, 21, 44, 57
Sisneros, Jose Rafael, 29
Sisneros, Juan Antonio, 48
Sisneros, Juana Maria (br), 30
Sisneros, Maria Bibiana, 29, 40
Sisneros, Maria Biviana, 32
Sisneros, Maria de la Lus, 21
Sisneros, Maria de la Lus (br), 44
Sisneros, Maria del Rosario, 54
Sisneros, Maria Gertrudes, 3
Sisneros, Maria Guadalupe, 33
Sisneros, Maria Juliana, 9
Sisneros, Maria Juliana (br), 57
Sisneros, Maria Manuela, 39, 57

Sisneros, Maria Teodora, 44, 56
Sisneros, Maria Tomasa, 47
Sisneros, Maria Ygnacia, 8
Sisneros, Pedro Antonio (gr), 32
Sisneros, Roman, 27, 31
Sisneros, Vibiana, 11
Sisneros, Viviana, 13
Suares, Maria Canuta, 28
Suares, Maria Casilda (br), 28
Suares, Pedro, 28
Suaso, Antonio, 3, 7, 39
Suaso, Concepcion, 39
Suaso, Concepsion, 33
Suaso, Jesus Maria (gr), 39
Suaso, Jose Miguel (gr), 42
Suaso, Juan Ysidro, 33
Suaso, Maria Concepcion, 39
Suaso, Ygnacio, 42
Suazo, Maria Gertrudis, 37

T

Tafoya, Maria Josefa, 8
Tageda, Antonio, 14
Tageda, Maria Josefa (br), 14
Telles, Maria, 16
Toledo, Maria Guadalupe, 15
Torres, Albino, 37
Torres, Alejandro, 7
Torres, Bernardo, 8, 37, 44
Torres, Carlos, 23, 37, 45
Torres, Francisco Antonio (gr), 9
Torres, Jose Bernardo, 9
Torres, Jose Maria (gr), 37
Torres, Josefa, 48
Torres, Juan Santos (gr), 44
Torres, Manuel Antonio (gr), 45
Torres, Manuel Gregorio, 9
Torres, Maria Paubla (br), 8
Torres, Maria Paula, 44
Torres, Maria Rita (br), 9
Torres, Micaela, 18
Trugillo, Acencio, 12, 19
Trugillo, Agustin, 3
Trugillo, Ana Maria, 15
Trugillo, Andres, 46

Trugillo, Anna Maria, 42
Trugillo, Antonia Josefa, 22
Trugillo, Antonio, 16
Trugillo, Antonio de Jesus (gr), 3
Trugillo, Balentia, 14
Trugillo, Bartolo, 15
Trugillo, Cerafina, 11
Trugillo, Concepcion, 36
Trugillo, Dolores, 8, 25
Trugillo, Domingo, 4, 5, 7, 8, 12, 16, 17, 22, 23, 24
Trugillo, Esteban, 41
Trugillo, Estefana, 41
Trugillo, Eusabio, 32
Trugillo, Faustin (gr), 45
Trugillo, Felipe de Jesus, 20
Trugillo, Felipe de Jesus (gr), 12
Trugillo, Francisco, 9, 11, 15, 21, 26
Trugillo, Francisco Antonio, 40, 52
Trugillo, Francisco Estevan (gr), 24
Trugillo, Getrudes, 54
Trugillo, Getrudis (br), 57
Trugillo, Jose, 32, 39, 51
Trugillo, Jose Albino (gr), 51
Trugillo, Jose Andres, 32
Trugillo, Jose Andres (gr), 38
Trugillo, Jose Antonio, 44
Trugillo, Jose Francisco, 45
Trugillo, Jose Francisco (gr), 16, 51
Trugillo, Jose Juan, 9
Trugillo, Jose Julian (gr), 36
Trugillo, Jose Luisano (gr), 37
Trugillo, Jose Manuel, 4, 8, 35
Trugillo, Jose Maria, 5, 8, 10, 37, 39, 46, 51
Trugillo, Jose Merced (gr), 54
Trugillo, Jose Miguel, 46
Trugillo, Jose Miguel (gr), 14, 46
Trugillo, Jose Modesto (gr), 8
Trugillo, Jose Paublo, 8
Trugillo, Jose Ramon, 53, 56
Trugillo, Jose Ysidro, 54
Trugillo, Juan, 19, 57
Trugillo, Juan Andres (gr), 39
Trugillo, Juan Antonio, 4, 11, 14
Trugillo, Juan Antonio (gr), 20, 28
Trugillo, Juan de Dios, 23, 25, 27, 39

Trugillo, Juan de Jesus, 38
Trugillo, Juan de Jesus (gr), 56
Trugillo, Juan de los Reyes (gr), 28
Trugillo, Juan Francisco, 17
Trugillo, Juan Nepomuceno (gr), 35
Trugillo, Juan Noverto (gr), 8
Trugillo, Juan Rafael, 56
Trugillo, Juan Simon, 16
Trugillo, Juan Ysidro (gr), 3
Trugillo, Julian, 15, 43
Trugillo, Julian de la Jesus (gr), 11
Trugillo, Lorenso, 7, 8, 9, 18
Trugillo, Lorenzo Antonio (gr), 39
Trugillo, Loreta, 8
Trugillo, Manuel Antonio (gr), 3
Trugillo, Manuel de los Dolores (gr), 9
Trugillo, Manuela, 19
Trugillo, Maria Ana (br), 20
Trugillo, Maria Antonia (br), 35, 41, 53
Trugillo, Maria Barbara, 36
Trugillo, Maria Bitalia, 38
Trugillo, Maria Cerafaina, 7
Trugillo, Maria Concepcion, 12
Trugillo, Maria Concepcion (br), 12
Trugillo, Maria Crisanta (br), 39
Trugillo, Maria de Jesus, 15
Trugillo, Maria de la Crus, 45
Trugillo, Maria de la Cruz, 57
Trugillo, Maria de la Lus, 36
Trugillo, Maria del Rosario, 8
Trugillo, Maria Dolores (br), 23, 53, 57
Trugillo, Maria Encanasion (br), 28
Trugillo, Maria Flora (br), 43
Trugillo, Maria Gertrudes, 23
Trugillo, Maria Gertrudes (br), 27
Trugillo, Maria Getrudis, 53, 54
Trugillo, Maria Guadalupe, 33
Trugillo, Maria Guadalupe (br), 9, 12, 19, 34
Trugillo, Maria Jasinta, 10, 37
Trugillo, Maria Josefa, 18, 24, 28, 31, 35, 52
Trugillo, Maria Josefa (br), 37
Trugillo, Maria Juana, 28, 45, 56
Trugillo, Maria Manuela, 12, 14, 28, 38, 41, 42, 53
Trugillo, Maria Manuela (br), 7, 15

Trugillo, Maria Nieves (br), 36
Trugillo, Maria Pasquala (br), 9
Trugillo, Maria Paubla (br), 52
Trugillo, Maria Rafaela, 5
Trugillo, Maria Ramona, 15
Trugillo, Maria Romuela, 7
Trugillo, Maria Serafina (br), 40
Trugillo, Maria Teresa, 34
Trugillo, Maria Trinidad (br), 21
Trugillo, Maria Ursula, 36
Trugillo, Maria Valentina, 32
Trugillo, Maria Ynes (br), 16
Trugillo, Maria Ysabel (br), 32
Trugillo, Martin Romualdo, 18
Trugillo, Martin Romualdo (gr), 17
Trugillo, Martina, 21
Trugillo, Miguel, 36
Trugillo, Nepomuceno, 6
Trugillo, Nicolas, 8, 18, 20, 24
Trugillo, Pablo, 6, 13, 25, 44
Trugillo, Pasquala, 14
Trugillo, Paublin, 12
Trugillo, Pedro, 12, 14, 24, 29, 38
Trugillo, Pedro Antonio, 7
Trugillo, Pedro Rafael (gr), 29
Trugillo, Poncisa, 56
Trugillo, Profero, 17, 27, 28
Trugillo, Profero (gr), 19
Trugillo, Profiro, 13
Trugillo, Rafael, 3, 4, 17, 20, 21, 24, 30, 32, 33, 34, 36, 37
Trugillo, Ramona, 17
Trugillo, Santiago, 10, 12, 14, 15, 31, 32, 33, 35, 36, 37, 51, 52, 54, 55, 57
Trugillo, Ygnacio, 7, 15, 23, 27, 34
Trujeques, Vicente, 39
Trujillo, Acension, 28
Trujillo, Bernardo (gr), 51
Trujillo, Biviana, 50
Trujillo, Blas, 49
Trujillo, Clemente, 49
Trujillo, Cleto (gr), 48
Trujillo, Francisco Estevan, 47
Trujillo, Guadalupe, 14
Trujillo, Jose Antonio (gr), 49
Trujillo, Jose Francisco (gr), 46

Trujillo, Jose Manuel, 47, 51
Trujillo, Juan Esteban (gr), 47
Trujillo, Juana Maria, 51
Trujillo, Manuel Gregorio (gr), 47
Trujillo, Maria Barbara, 49
Trujillo, Maria Consepcion (br), 50
Trujillo, Maria de la Cruz (br), 51
Trujillo, Maria de la Luz (br), 47
Trujillo, Maria Josefa (br), 46
Trujillo, Maria Loreta, 48
Trujillo, Maria Paubla (br), 28
Trujillo, Maria Rosa, 4
Trujillo, Maria Rosalia, 50
Trujillo, Maria Ygnacia, 49
Trujillo, Maria Ygnes, 50
Trujillo, Pablo, 16, 30, 48, 49, 51
Trujillo, Pedro, 48, 50, 51
Trujillo, Profiro, 9
Trujillo, Salbador, 49
Trujillo, Ysidro, 47, 51
Truxillo, Barbara Antonia, 1
Truxillo, Bernanda, 27
Truxillo, Jose Juan, 2, 27
Truxillo, Jose Maria Santiago (gr), 27
Truxillo, Jose Pablo, 1, 26
Truxillo, Juan de Jesus (gr), 26
Truxillo, Juan Ramon (gr), 27
Truxillo, Leon, 26
Truxillo, Maria Atanacia, 1
Truxillo, Maria Barbara, 2
Truxillo, Maria Brigida, 2
Truxillo, Maria Jacinta (br), 2
Truxillo, Mariano, 26, 27
Truxillo, Miguel, 2
Truxillo, Nasario (gr), 26
Truxillo, Pedro, 2, 3, 26
Truxillo, Ygnacio, 1

U

Ulibarri, Ana Maria, 51
Ulibarri, Candelaria, 57
Ulibarri, Juan, 55
Uraibali, Gregorio, 9
Uribali, Maria Concepcion, 4
Urribali, Gregorio, 23

Urribali, Jose, 10
Urribali, Manuel de Jesus (gr), 9
Urtado, Antonio de la Cruz (gr), 12
Urtado, Antonio Nerio, 55
Urtado, Dolores, 12
Urtado, Jasinto, 12
Urtado, Maria Dolores, 25
Urtado, Maria Ines (br), 55

V

Valdes, Ana Maria (br), 34, 36
Valdes, Andrea (br), 18
Valdes, Antonia Rosa, 19
Valdes, Antonio, 38, 40, 50
Valdes, Antonio (gr), 55
Valdes, Antonio de Jesus (gr), 36
Valdes, Antonio Jose, 34
Valdes, Antonio Nerio, 45
Valdes, Bernardo, 21
Valdes, Esuebio, 33
Valdes, Eusebio, 36
Valdes, Feliciana, 22
Valdes, Francisca, 41
Valdes, Francisco, 10, 37, 53
Valdes, German, 27, 33, 51
Valdes, Guadalupe, 55
Valdes, Jesus Merced (gr), 53
Valdes, Joae Miguel, 38
Valdes, Jose, 32
Valdes, Jose Deciderio (gr), 42
Valdes, Jose Eusebio (gr), 50
Valdes, Jose Francisco, 19
Valdes, Jose Gabriel, 39
Valdes, Jose Gabriel (gr), 26
Valdes, Jose Geronimo (gr), 40
Valdes, Jose Manuel, 27, 35, 36, 51, 55
Valdes, Jose Maria (gr), 20, 24, 40
Valdes, Jose Nasario (gr), 33
Valdes, Jose Ramon, 19, 21
Valdes, Jose Ygnacio, 40, 52
Valdes, Josefa, 37
Valdes, Juan Antonio, 37
Valdes, Juan Nepomuceno, 34, 50
Valdes, Juan Nepomuseno, 36
Valdes, Juan Nepomuseno (gr), 35

Valdes, Juan Pablo (gr), 32
Valdes, Juan Pedro, 20
Valdes, Juan Ymilio, 57
Valdes, Juan Ysidro, 29
Valdes, Juana Catarina, 49
Valdes, Juana Josefa, 25
Valdes, Manuel, 24, 34
Valdes, Maria Agapita (br), 51
Valdes, Maria Alta Gracia (br), 52
Valdes, Maria Antonia, 28
Valdes, Maria Antonia (br), 44
Valdes, Maria Antonia Vegnina (br), 56
Valdes, Maria Bitazia (br), 38
Valdes, Maria de la Crus (br), 19
Valdes, Maria de la Lus, 46, 54
Valdes, Maria de la Luz, 47, 54
Valdes, Maria de los Reyes, 24
Valdes, Maria de Trinidad (br), 38
Valdes, Maria del Refugio, 54
Valdes, Maria Equipula, 51
Valdes, Maria Esquipula, 39
Valdes, Maria Estefana, 46
Valdes, Maria Estefana (br), 22, 39
Valdes, Maria Ferminia (br), 57
Valdes, Maria Francisca, 33
Valdes, Maria Joaefa, 45
Valdes, Maria Josefa, 45
Valdes, Maria Josefa (br), 40, 45
Valdes, Maria Juana, 20, 30, 49
Valdes, Maria Lidubina (br), 43
Valdes, Maria Lucia, 44
Valdes, Maria Luisa (br), 21
Valdes, Maria Manuela, 28, 29, 34, 54
Valdes, Maria Manuela (br), 29, 41
Valdes, Maria Micaela, 36
Valdes, Maria Nicolasa (br), 33
Valdes, Maria Regina, 37
Valdes, Maria Rita, 34
Valdes, Maria Rosalia, 26
Valdes, Maria Rufina, 46, 56
Valdes, Maria Rufina (br), 21
Valdes, Maria Rugina, 45
Valdes, Maria Soledad (br), 33
Valdes, Maria Ygnacia, 18, 46, 53
Valdes, Maria Ygnacia (br), 37, 53
Valdes, Mariano, 31, 32, 33, 46

Valdes, Miguel, 43
Valdes, Pedro Acencio (gr), 20
Valdes, Pedro Antonio, 52
Valdes, Rafael, 26, 33, 48, 49
Valdes, Ramon, 22, 56
Valdes, Reyes, 41
Valdes, Santiago, 42
Valdes, Silberio (gr), 46
Valdes, Simon, 53
Valdes, Tomas, 18
Valdes, Trinidad, 37
Valdes, Usebio, 20
Valdez, Maria de Jesus, 32
Valdez, Maria Petrona, 29
Valdez, Rafael (gr), 29
Vallejo, Maria Guadalupe, 56
Varela, Jesus Maria, 9, 20, 53, 54, 55, 56, 57, 58
Varela, Jose Guadalupe (gr), 57
Varela, Jose Manuel (gr), 28
Varela, Maria Arntonia, 14
Varela, Tomas, 57
Vargas, Jose, 54
Vargas, Maria Rosalia (br), 54
Varos, Maria de la Cruz, 13
Vasques, Maria de la Lus (br), 26
Velard, Jose Miguel, 21
Velarde, Jose Vicente Faustin (gr), 21
Velarde, Juan Luis, 34
Velarde, Maria Encarnacion, 26
Velarde, Maria Tiodora (br), 34
Velasques, Antonio Matias (gr), 52
Velasques, Joaquin, 18, 21, 26
Velasques, Jose, 26, 55
Velasques, Jose Maria (gr), 26
Velasques, Maria Andrea (br), 55
Velasques, Maria Concepcion, 53
Velasques, Maria Concepcion de, 41
Velasques, Maria Josefa, 19
Velasques, Maria Manuela (br), 55
Velasques, Maria Salome (br), 18
Velasques, Mateo, 55
Velasques, Ygnacio, 52
Velasquez, Juan de Esquipula (gr), 20
Velasquez, Maria Concepcion, 40
Velasquez, Maria Josefa, 25

Velasquez, Maria Manuela (br), 52
Velasquez, Ygnacio, 52
Venavides, Francisco Estevan (gr), 15
Venavides, Jose Antonio, 15
Venavides, Ysavel, 54
Vialpando, Maria de la Lus, 41
Vialpando, Maria Josefa, 42
Vialpando, Maria Manuela, 43
Vialpando, Maria Rita, 54
Vigil, Acencion, 44
Vigil, Ana Maria (br), 19
Vigil, Ana Maria de los Dolores (br), 20
Vigil, Angela, 32
Vigil, Antonia, 2
Vigil, Antonio, 22, 34
Vigil, Antonio Maria Narsiso (gr), 43
Vigil, Bautista, 49
Vigil, Benito (gr), 27
Vigil, Faustin, 19, 27, 48
Vigil, Francisco, 32, 34, 49, 51
Vigil, Francisco Esteban, 43
Vigil, Francisco Estevan, 7
Vigil, Grabriel, 3
Vigil, Jesus, 28
Vigil, Jose Francisco, 1, 11, 31, 55
Vigil, Jose Gregorio (gr), 55
Vigil, Jose Manuel, 20, 36, 45, 46, 56
Vigil, Jose Manuel (gr), 20, 37, 56
Vigil, Juan, 11, 42, 57
Vigil, Juan Angel, 56
Vigil, Juan de Jesus, 20
Vigil, Juan Maria, 33
Vigil, Maria Alta Gracia, 8

Vigil, Maria Antonia, 43
Vigil, Maria Asencion (br), 11
Vigil, Maria de la Lus, 11, 14
Vigil, Maria de la Luz (br), 42
Vigil, Maria Gregoria, 48
Vigil, Maria Juana, 57
Vigil, Maria Juana (br), 48
Vigil, Maria Madalena, 24
Vigil, Maria Rafaela, 10
Vigil, Maria Ramona (br), 56
Vigil, Maria Reyes, 44
Vigil, Maria Rita, 10
Vigil, Maria Rosa, 4, 34
Vigil, Maria Salome, 33, 43
Vigil, Maria Serafina, 32
Vigil, Maria Serafina (br), 50
Vigil, Maria Soledad, 34
Vigil, Maria Tomasa Casimira (br), 3
Vigil, Matias, 43
Vigil, Paubla, 14
Vigil, Pedro, 50
Vigil, Rafael, 48
Vigil, Ramon, 37
Vigil, Serafina, 39
Vijil, Jose Manuel, 48
Villalpando, Maria Josefa, 27
Villalpando, Maria Rita, 47
Villanueva, Maria de Jesus, 13
Villapando, Maria Rita, 8

Z

Zalazar, Jose Benito, 44

www.ingramcontent.com/pod-product-compliance
Lightning Source LLC
Chambersburg PA
CBHW080647270326
41928CB00017B/3228